The Early Drug Courts

Drugs, Health, and Social Policy Series

Edited by James A. Inciardi

University of Delaware

About This Series . . .

The Sage ***Drugs, Health, and Social Policy Series*** provides students and professionals in the fields of substance abuse, AIDS, public health, and criminal justice access to current research, programs, and policy issues particular to their specialties. Each volume focuses on a topic of national significance.

1. ***Drugs and Crime in Lifestyle Perspective***
   Glenn D. Walters
2. ***Policing Places With Drug Problems***
   Lorraine Green
3. ***Drug Control and the Courts***
   James A. Inciardi, Duane C. McBride, & James E. Rivers
4. ***Crack Cocaine, Crime, and Women***
   Sue Mahan
5. ***Cocaine-Exposed Infants***
   James A. Inciardi, Hilary L. Surratt, & Christine A. Saum
6. ***Heroin in the Age of Crack-Cocaine***
   James A. Inciardi & Lana D. Harrison
7. ***The Early Drug Courts***
   W. Clinton Terry, III

The Early Drug Courts

Case Studies in Judicial Innovation

W. Clinton Terry, III
Editor

Drugs, Health, and Social Policy Series
Volume 7

SAGE Publications
International Educational and Professional Publisher
Thousand Oaks London New Delhi

For information:

SAGE Publications, Inc.
2455 Teller Road
Thousand Oaks, California 91320
E-mail: order@sagepub.com

SAGE Publications Ltd.
6 Bonhill Street
London EC2A 4PU
United Kingdom

SAGE Publications India Pvt. Ltd.
M-32 Market
Greater Kailash I
New Delhi 110 048 India

Printed in the United States of America

Library of Congress Cataloging-in-Publication Data

Main Entry Under Title:

The early drug courts: Case studies in judicial innovation /
edited by W. Clinton Terry, III.
p. cm. — (Drugs, health, and social policy series; 7)
Includes bibliographical references and index.
ISBN 0-7619-0723-8 (cloth: acid-free paper)
ISBN 0-7619-0724-6 (pbk.: acid-free paper)
1. Drug courts—United States. 2. Drug abuse—Treatment—Law and legislation—United States. I. Terry, W. Clinton. II. Series.
KF3890 .E17 1998
345.73'0277—ddc21 98-25361

This book is printed on acid-free paper.

99 00 01 02 03 04 05 7 6 5 4 3 2 1

Acquiring Editor: C. Terry Hendrix
Editorial Assistant: Fiona Lyon
Production Editor: Denise Santoyo
Typesetter: Christina M. Hill
Indexer: Juniee Oneida

CONTENTS

Acknowledgments

There are many people to recognize for their help in preparing this book, but none are more important than the authors of the articles appearing in it. John S. Goldkamp, Elizabeth Piper Deschenes, Rebecca D. Petersen, Brooke Bedrick, Jerome H. Skolnick, and Steven Belenko graciously agreed to write pieces describing the organization and purpose of the drug courts they have studied, along with the results of their evaluations of how well these courts have worked. Judge Jeff Tauber, formerly of the Oakland Drug Court, now President of the National Association of Drug Court Professionals, was helpful in providing materials and assistance in completing the chapter on the Oakland Drug Court. During the inception and completion of this book, I received encouragement and support from David Bergwall, Director of the School of Policy Management at Florida International University. C. Terry Hendrix, Senior Editor at Sage Publications, was not only receptive to the idea of producing a book on the early drug courts but provided support during each stage of its development, as did his assistant Fiona Lyon and others from the Sage organization. There are many people with whom I have worked during the course of my research into drug court issues, who have shaped my views and those reflected in this book. David Choate, Executive Director of Broward County

Substance Abuse, lured me into the evaluation of Broward County's Drug Court, while Guy Wheeler, Director of the Broward County Drug Court Treatment Program, and Marie Reynolds, who was Executive Director of the Broward County Addiction Recovery Center at the time I collected data, smoothed my entrance into their treatment world and its issues so that I was able to collect and understand the information needed to track and evaluate client progress. The enthusiasm of Judge Robert Fogan, Broward's first Drug Court judge, was both inspirational and infectious. The dedication and hard work of the treatment counselors and staff, especially Phil Madan, Pearlie Spencer, Elaine Hammond, and Carmen Jones, who kindly tolerated my endless questions and requests for "just this one more piece of information" helped make my work more manageable and understandable. There were also numerous judicial and county officials who provided support when needed—Commissioner John Hart, Assistant to the County Administrator Pete Corwin, Chief Assistant State Attorney Ralph Ray, Clerk of the Broward County, Florida, Seventeenth Judicial Circuit Court Robert Lockwood (who provided a list of first-time cocaine drug offenders from which a comparison group was selected, and Leslie Monteith and Julie Poole from Pretrial Services who determined who was Drug Court eligible from among the list of offenders provided by the Clerk's Office. Special thanks go to Pat Voss and Lisa Hauser for the hundreds of hours spent making sense of court records and for translating and inputting the data in machine-readable form. Finally, I would like to thank all the drug court professionals I have met at meetings and elsewhere and to my students, who by now have probably grown tired of my droning on about the value of drug courts within American jurisprudence.

Foreword

When the first drug court opened in Miami, Florida, a decade ago, little did its planners and participants dream that a modest local experiment would catalyze an international movement. The building blocks of that first court—common sense, collaboration, and an eagerness to share the lessons of both success and failure with other jurisdictions—were critical to its success, and they were shared by the early courts that followed.

This book tells the stories of the pioneers of the drug court movement. It tells the stories of individuals who, frustrated with an unresponsive system, embraced change at great risk. Today's many drug courts owe a great debt to the history created by these few. As drug courts increase rapidly across America and gain an international footing, it is gratifying to see that their efforts retain the passion, commitment, and camaraderie that marked the work that first brought drug courts to reality.

The pioneer courts that are the focus of this study were developed at a time when the nation was waging its full-scale "war" on drugs. Congress and state legislatures were responding to growing numbers of drug offenders with mandatory minimum-sentencing laws; prosecutors and police were conducting drug sweeps that resulted in mass arrests; and the nation's courts were hard at work developing fast-track mechanisms to dispose of rapidly growing caseloads as quickly as possible. In this highly charged atmosphere, prevention and treatment were seen as soft and potentially dangerous approaches by many policy makers, especially those at the highest federal levels: programs competing for funding that officials felt would be better spent on enforcement and interdiction.

The first drug courts sought to confront addiction head on. They sought to do more than simply process criminal cases generated by addiction; they sought to change behavior and restore individuals to a productive role in society. This seemingly straightforward goal for the criminal justice system—treating addiction while offenders are under the coercive power of the court—was met with disdain by funding agencies, policy makers, the media, and practitioners in traditional courts, who viewed the first drug court judges, public defenders, prosecutors, providers, and administrators as having missed the point of the war on drugs.

Judges were not viewed as problem solvers; prosecutors and defenders were considered adversaries, not collaborators; providers were believed to work best in isolation, untainted by the concerns of justice systems; and administrators, operating within strict fiscal boundaries, were not in the business of funding treatments or treatment enhancements, such as acupuncture, that they considered to be voodoo-like practices. Even drug testing, now an essential component of drug courts, was seen as a tool not to move clients toward sobriety but to trigger punitive sanctions, such as incarceration, against them.

Traditional courts, funders, and policy makers were also hostile to the idea that drug-involved clients needed assistance in the courtroom for social service needs such as a decent job, housing, or education. Meeting those needs, they believed, was in the domain of others, not the nation's justice systems.

The first drug courts not only persevered against these odds, and without financial or moral support from any quarter of federal government, but spread the promise of their new approach to communities throughout the country. Such has been the extraordinary growth of this concept that it is difficult now to imagine that only 10 years ago, a single drug court existed, struggling to gain acceptance and funding.

What was seen by many in the early days of drug courts as a radical approach to addiction within the criminal justice system can now be seen as the first significant step toward change. This thoughtful and well-researched volume—the first book-length academic study of the drug court movement—documents how remarkable and difficult that step was. The court's legacy, its emphasis on problem solving rather than case processing, is one that will influence our nation's concept of justice.

Timothy J. Murray
Director, Planning and Policy Division
Bureau of Justice Assistance
Office of Justice Programs
U.S. Department of Justice

1. Judicial Change and Dedicated Treatment Courts: Case Studies in Innovation

W. Clinton Terry, III

There is something new in the courts of America. They have been taking a new look at how the criminal justice system handles drug offenders. With the press of drug cases on judicial dockets, judges have sought alternative means to expedite cases through the system. Although expedited case-management strategies and specialized drug courts helped process cases faster and allowed judges more time to deal with serious felony cases, drug offenders continued to reoffend and reappear before the judiciary, often in the same courtroom. From these beginnings, the new paradigm of dedicated drug treatment courts arose.

Dedicated drug courts bring treatment into the courts and the courts into treatment. Rather than being concerned with speeding up the process, dedicated drug treatment courts, as they have come to be known, are willing to hold onto drug offenders for a longer period of time, providing offenders with treatment, with the intention that fewer, in the long run, would reappear in the courtroom. Not only would this have a long-term impact on reducing the number of drug cases coming into court, it would also have the positive effect of reducing the level of crime committed by these drug offenders, either as the result of their subsequent purchase or possession of drugs or as the result of the crimes they might commit to support their habit.

Dedicated treatment courts have been tremendously successful. Based on a 1992 survey, Inciardi, McBride, and Rivers (1996, p. 74) predicted that by early 1992 there would be about 420 drug courts nationwide with another 1,000 jurisdictions or more considering them. Although a bit optimistic, these estimates were on target in terms of the phenomenal growth drug courts have experienced in recent years. According to a General Accounting Office (GAO, 1997, p. 8) survey, 42 drug courts were started between 1989 and 1994. Since then, 4 have closed and 123 more have started, bringing the total to 161 as of the end of March 1997. Moreover, an additional 154 drug courts are at varying stages of planning. Drug courts are operating in 38 states, the District of Columbia, and Puerto Rico. About 40% of the drug court programs are located in California and Florida. More recently, the National Association of Drug Court Professionals reported that more than 300 drug courts are in operation, with several hundred more expected to become operational by June 1998.[1] This impressive growth rate has been made possible, at least in part, by the availability of federal and state funds. Since the beginning in 1989, more than $125 million have been allotted to develop drug courts throughout the country (GAO, 1997, p. 9).

This volume is an extension and to a degree an elaboration of *Drug Control and the Courts* (Inciardi et al., 1996), Volume 3 in Sage's Drug, Health, and Social Policy Series. The earlier volume focuses on the relationship between drugs and crime, tracing the history and development of drug control efforts as they relate to American courts. It ends with a discussion of dedicated drug treatment courts and their immediate predecessors, differentiated case management, expedited drug case management courts, and specialized courts that dealt only with drug cases. The present volume, *The Early Drug Courts: Case Studies in Judicial Innovation,* examines the history, development, and treatment programs of the five earliest drug courts in the United States. Its focus is less on the linkage between drugs and crime than it is on different attempts to bring the treatment community into the sanctioning and supervisory processes of the courts. It may be argued that these efforts are among the most innovative strategies occurring within the American court system during the past several decades. The rapid growth of these courts is a testament to the seriousness with which local communities view the drug problem that has been growing since the 1970s and 1980s. It is also a testament to the ability of local government and courts to adapt to changing circumstances and needs.

The Drug Problem[2]

There is little question that drug offenses have increased over the years. The National Survey of Drug Abuse estimates that 12.8 million people age 12 years or older used illicit drugs during the month prior to being interviewed in 1995. The cost of these illegal drug practices—costs related to lost work productivity, illness, accidents, crime, law enforcement, and health care—was in excess of $100 billion (Substance Abuse and Mental Health Services Administration, 1996, p. 2). The Office of National Drug Control Policy (1996, p. 2) estimated that federal, state, and local governments spend $30 billion a year combatting illegal drug use and trafficking. In addition, the Office put the social cost of illegal drug use at $67 billion, mostly the result of drug-related crime. Each year, more than 1 million people are arrested for drug-related offenses, and 20,000 Americans die as the result of illicit drug abuse.

In 1981, President Reagan abandoned the government's reliance on treatment and prevention in favor of strengthening law enforcement efforts to reduce drug supplies, in conjunction with a policy of zero tolerance for dealers and users (Falco, 1994, p. 6). This increased law enforcement emphasis led to more arrests, prosecutions, and incarcerations. According to the FBI's Uniform Crime Report (Cooper & Trotter, 1994b, p. 84; U.S. Department of Justice, 1990, p. 176), arrests for drug abuse violations increased from 377,175 in 1980 to 852,105 in 1989. This was an increase of 125%, compared to a 18.9% increase in the total crime index over the same period.

The impact of these arrests on the courts was predictable. In 26 urban courts, drug-related caseloads increased about 56% between 1983 and 1987 (Goerdt & Martin, 1989). Already saturated, courts were unable to handle these increases; consequently, case processing slowed (Goerdt, Lomvardias, & Gallas, 1990; Goerdt & Martin, 1989).

Responses to increased caseloads focused on improving court efficiency and were of three general types (Belenko & Dumanovsky, 1993; Smith, Davis, & Goretsky, 1991). First, differentiated case management and/or expedited drug case management attempted to evaluate cases early in the judicial process to place them on appropriate tracks and watch them carefully as they proceeded through the court system. These efforts often led to cases being processed more quickly. Second, specialized drug courts were created to handle only drug cases. Not only did these courts expedite cases through the system, but judges also became experts in trying drug cases (Goldkamp, 1994, p. 3; Smith, Davis, & Lurigio, 1994, p. 115). In addition, these specialized courts were able to give more attention to drug cases, which had often been pushed to the bottom of court calendars in favor of cases involving more serious violent offenders (Smith et al., 1994, p. 115). Third, dedicated drug treatment courts came into existence (Belenko & Dumanovsky, 1993; Goldkamp & Weiland, 1993). Although similar to specialized drug courts, dedicated drug treatment courts focused on treatment provided by addiction specialists working closely with the court. Within these courts, the traditional adversarial relationship between prosecution and defense was replaced by a collegial team approach. In addition, people diverted into treatment were monitored by the judiciary, thus making the court an integral part of the treatment process itself (Goldkamp, 1994, p. 4).

The Old and the New

Although there are many differences between drug courts, the provision of treatment and the monitoring of treatment by the judiciary stands at the core of most. The more traditional method of handling drug offenders differed little from handling other types of offenses. Traditional handling of drug offenders focused on the offense rather than on the underlying addiction.

Under the traditional model of case processing, offenders are booked, often at the county jail. If the offense is bondable, they can be released until first appearance. If no bond is available or the person is unable to post bond, they are held in jail until they can appear before the court, generally within a day or two of arrest. When they appear before the court, offenders are informed of the charges against them; indigence and legal representation are determined as is pretrial release, where applicable; and an arraignment date is set. Those individuals who are unable to post bond or who have not already done so and those people ineligible for pretrial release or release on their own recognizance are returned to jail to await arraignment. If they plead not guilty at arraignment, a trial date is set; otherwise, in most cases, sentence is imposed at arraignment.

Despite the existence of speedy trial statutes in most states, substance abuse offenders may wait for the better part of a month before arraignment and even longer before trial. If they remain in jail, their substance abuse will be greatly curtailed, although perhaps not eliminated. People who are released, however, are free to pursue their prior drug habits. The difference between the traditional approach to processing drug offenders and what happens in dedicated drug treatment courts lies in the focus on treatment and the speed with which cases are sent to treatment.

Dedicated drug treatment courts, where appropriate, attempt to intervene in the lives of individuals as soon after arrest as possible. The logic of this swift intervention rests on an attempt to capitalize on the trauma of arrest and booking to convince people they are in need of treatment. This effect is often lost if the time from arrest to treatment is overly long. Hence, in many drug court jurisdictions, people arrested for drug offenses, often first-time offenders, appear before the drug court, rather than the lower court scheduled to hear initial appearances on that particular day. All people who are eligible for drug court could be entered into drug court that very day. They will, of course, come back to the court for arraignment and for final disposition of the case, if need be, and for regular status hearings before the presiding judge. If the person successfully completes the treatment program, as determined by the treatment providers and the court, the charges against that person may be dropped if the drug court is a diversionary court and/or sentences may be shortened or dismissed if the drug court is a postadjudication court. In either case, the drug courts are able to start working with the drug offender quite soon after entering into the criminal justice system.

Judicial Reform and Innovation

The structure of local government in the United States favors home rule; consequently, the history of the American judicature is filled with a diversity of lower and trial courts at the local level. Even within single states, court organization has often exhibited great variation. Such variation has led court watchers to comment on the inefficiency and inadequacy of the judicial system (Neubauer, 1996,

p. 54; President's Commission on Law Enforcement and the Administration of Justice, 1967; cf. Ashman, 1975).

In reforming this diversity of courts, attempts have been made to create a system of single county courts, each having one trial court. Such reforms have led to the creation of appellate courts, standing above county courts, and state supreme courts standing above appellate courts (Berkson & Carbon, 1978; National Institute of Justice, 1984; Rubin, 1984; Tarr, 1981). In general, each state court system would have a central form of administration, rule making, budgeting, and finance (Hudzik, 1985; Stout, 1986). Reform along these lines resembles classical organizational models, focusing on rational planning, chain of command, and coordination (Gallas, 1979; Hudzik, 1985; Lamber & Luskin, 1992); it has met with considerable success within the United States. However, the ties of the judiciary and the criminal justice system to local government have prevented complete unification (Baar, 1993).

To a considerable degree, criminal justice remains largely a local affair. Sheriffs are elected locally. Municipal police departments serve their local communities, and their chiefs report to local government. Law enforcement agencies decide what laws receive the most attention. These decisions often reflect community desires and help determine who enters the court system. Most judges, as well as state attorneys and public defenders, are elected; hence, they are sensitive and responsive to local issues and sentiments. Prosecutors and defense attorneys, as well as court clerks and other court personnel, also have local roots and thus reflect local behaviors and attitudes. Even those who come to a local court from outside develop, after a while, attitudes and behaviors reflecting the attitudes and behaviors of the dominant courthouse culture (Church, 1985, pp. 449-518; Fleming, Nardulli, & Eisenstein, 1992; Jacobs, 1991, pp. 211-213; Neubauer, 1996, pp. 7-76; Wice, 1985). This weight of local tradition and organization often means that for significant criminal justice change to succeed, it must have the support of the major criminal justice players within the community. In particular, judicial change must have the support of its judges. As Provine and Seron (1995) note,

> The organization of American courts shields trial level judges from the efforts of outsiders to impose change. The irony is that the American court system, more insulated than most from hierarchical and direct political controls, may be more nurturing than most toward innovations that judges themselves deem appropriate. (p. 510)

Dedicated Drug Courts as Judicial Innovation

What is innovative about dedicated drug treatment courts? There are a number of answers, but two appear most prominent. First, dedicated drug treatment courts have turned traditional judges into substance abuse problem solvers, to borrow a phrase from community-oriented policing. As problem solvers, judges are less concerned about violations of the law, although that remains a concern, than they are about the underlying reasons bringing people into the courtroom in the first place. This focus upon underlying reasons translates into developing alternatives within their judicial prerogative to deal with these problems while, at the same time, administering state sanctions against the illegal behavior that brought the people into court. By bringing treatment into the courtroom, an effort is made to modify offenders' substance-abusing behavior, thus reducing their level of future criminality and in turn reducing the frequency with which they reappear in the court. Second, dedicated drug treatment courts develop innovative partnerships able to deal with the needs of the criminal justice system and the difficulties associated with addictive behavior. Rather than operating alone, as one agency within the criminal justice system, dedicated drug treatment courts reach out into the community to form partnerships with community treatment organizations. Rather than doing battle to determine the guilt or innocence of the defendant, treatment service providers work alongside pretrial services, probation officers, prosecutors, defense counsel, and judges, all of them making up a collaborative team that focuses on the treatment progress of offenders. Of course, monitoring treatment progress includes monitoring conforming behavior in the community.

Problem Solving: The notion of problem solving in criminal justice has gained popularity along with community-oriented policing. Numerous police administrators have noticed that they respond to many calls from the same areas. Regardless of what they do, they still receive calls from these areas. In short, they fail to deal with the underlying problems that are generating these calls for service. What some police departments have discovered is that when they focus on solving these underlying problems—as well as making arrests where necessary—fewer crimes, arrests, and calls for assistance have come from these locations.

A similar shift in thinking appears to have occurred in the courts. Rather than adjudicating the same substance-abusing offender over and over again, courts have adopted dedicated drug treatment courts as a means of getting at the underlying addiction causing their substance-abusing behavior. By focusing on people with substance abuse problems, dedicated drug treatment courts are less concerned with how many people are processed through the system within a certain period of time than they are with providing a remedy to the addiction and related problems that have brought the defendants into court. In general, the primary goals of drug treatment courts are not to prosecute and punish, although they do that, too, but to provide alternatives to drug offenders in dealing head on with their addiction. This is done by (a) providing an understanding of addiction and teaching offenders about effective relapse prevention measures, (b) assisting in the development of better living and work skills, and (c) developing attitudes and behaviors conducive to avoiding a return to the criminal justice system.

Partnerships as a Collaborative Model of Justice: Dedicated drug treatment goals are developed in partnership with local government and other criminal justice agencies, as well as community treatment providers. The partnerships develop a mutual sense of mission and collaboration. These partnerships are greatly aided by the flexibility of the local courts. Being grounded in the political and social organization of the community, the courts provide a vehicle through which drug court goals may be molded into a workable whole.

Because most dedicated drug treatment courts view substance abuse as a disease, the crime of possession and purchase of illicit substances requires treatment, not incarceration. This view requires the courtroom players to become team players rather than client advocates. As Goldkamp (1994) states, "The drug court is really the result of a special collaborative effort, a team approach: first among criminal justice actors and treatment providers . . . [then by] other social services and community organizations" (p. 7; cf. GAO, 1995, p. 15). The implementation of this collaborative model involves a transformation of traditional judicial rules. These changes are summarized by Cooper and Trotter (1994a):

> Although the prosecutor and defense counsel are present at most Drug Court proceedings, the purpose of each hearing is to promote the treatment and rehabilitation of the defendant and it is to this end that all parties direct their effort. The prosecutor agrees to defer prosecution of cases that might be easy convictions; the defense counsel forgoes arguing motions which might be dispositive and the Drug Court judge abandons

his/her sanctioning role and, instead, motivates defendants to enter treatment and often inspires them with the court's confidence that they can rehabilitate themselves and rid themselves of drug dependency. When in subsequent status hearings, it becomes apparent that the defendant is not progressing satisfactorily, the remedy is usually to enhance treatment—not to litigate. (p. 27)

The collaborative model of justice that is embraced by drug courts places the judge at the center (Goldkamp, 1994, pp. iv, 7). Proceedings often become a dialogue between the judge and the other participants. The goal is to provide psychological support to the defendant and to instill individual responsibility for recovery as much as it is to keep the participants within the narrower confines of programmatic roles and expectations.

The Early Dedicated Drug Treatment Courts

The early dedicated drug treatment courts depicted in this volume are offered as illustrations of judicial innovation involving problem solving and collaborative partnerships. They are the dedicated drug treatment courts of Miami (Dade County), Florida; Oakland (Alameda County), California; Fort Lauderdale (Broward County), Florida; Phoenix (Maricopa County), Arizona; and Portland (Multnomah County), Oregon. These are five of the earliest treatment courts in the United States. To a very real extent, they served as models for many of the courts that followed, just as the innovations of the many courts following them served, in turn, as models for subsequent courts.

Some of these early courts were entirely local in creation and funding. Others came into existence with the assistance of external (i.e., federal) funding. Three of these courts were diversionary courts; two of them were postadjudication courts. The impetus of change often came from the courts; however, in at least one case, Maricopa County, change was triggered by the needs of the community probation department. The partnerships that arose to provide the services typical of dedicated drug treatment courts varied from a few individuals and agencies to the inclusion of a full range of judicial officers and community service providers. These different arrangements attest to the flexibility and resourcefulness of judicial organizations at the local level.

Miami Drug Court

John Goldkamp's chapter, "The Origin of the Treatment Drug Court in Miami," succinctly recounts the goals, problems, and development of Miami's drug court. Being the first dedicated drug treatment court in the United States, it became the model other drug courts used as a pattern. The Miami Drug Court arose out the frustrations of the late 1980s in South Florida, brought on by an increasingly difficult drug problem, especially the use of crack cocaine, and the resultant increase in court cases. Against this background, the Chief Administrative Judge of the Eleventh Judicial Circuit of Florida, Judge Gerald T. Wetherington, asked Judge Herbert Klein to recommend solutions to the judicial crisis that was upon them. Out of this initiative arose the concept of a team of criminal justice actors working together to supervise and encourage the progress of a defendant entering a treatment program as a condition of deferred prosecution.

Miami's experiment was premised on the notion that the interests and needs of justice were compatible with the interests and needs of treatment, and that acting together, public officials could improve the lives of drug offenders, positively affect public safety, and reduce court caseloads. The combination of criminal justice and treatment goals in a single program provided the dynamic fulcrum around which Miami's drug court, as well as many subsequent drug courts, revolved. The evaluation of Miami's drug court employed several comparison groups and found that 83% of the people eligible for drug court actually entered treatment and about 60 percent could be classified as achieving a favorable program outcome. After 18 months, program graduates had been rearrested less frequently than a sample of felony defendants processed through the circuit court at the same time as the treatment defendants, and less frequently than a sample of felony defendants processed through the circuit court prior to the implementation of the drug court. Drug court participants who were rearrested were detained after longer intervals than either of the other two samples of felony defendants.

The Oakland Drug Court

In "From 'Treatment' to 'Justice,' " Brooke Bedrick and Jerome H. Skolnick describe how Judge Jeff Tauber, faced with very few resources, struggled to turn Oakland's expedited drug court into a treatment drug court so that he could better monitor the drug treatment into which he was diverting first-time drug offenders. He succeeded; Oakland's Drug Court (i.e., The Oakland-Piedmont-Emeryville Municipal Drug Court)—otherwise known as Oakland's FIRST program (Fast, Intensive, Report, Supervision, and Treatment)—officially began receiving defendants in January 1991.

Oakland is located in the midst of a major metropolitan area. Like Miami, Oakland faced an increasing drug problem in the middle to late 1980s, including addiction to cocaine and heroin. Like all the drug courts profiled in this volume, Oakland's drug court involved a flexible and innovative partnership among criminal justice agencies and treatment service providers and counselors.

Contingency contracts and graduated sanctions were the hallmarks of Oakland's earliest dedicated drug treatment court. Contracts between the treatment court and the defendant outlined the expectations at each phase of the program. The contracts were built on a point system that allowed an individual the opportunity to reduce the length of probation by accumulating a certain number of points. Should nonconforming behavior occur, graduated sanctions were applied. These sanctions ranged from spending the morning in the jury box to observe and learn from what was happening to others as they appeared before the court to being placed in custody for a few days.

The assessment of the Oakland drug court shows the number of people reporting to court for eligibility hearings increased; more people were granted diversion; twice as many completed the program; and there were lower levels of rearrest among those entering the FIRST diversion program than among those placed on diversion from the expedited drug court in 1990. These in-house findings were supported by a study from the National Center for State Courts (1996).

In 1996, Oakland's FIRST program was merged with the postadjudication program of Superior Court drug court program. Although the two courts continue to run their own programs, the policies of these courts have shifted from an antirecidivism policy; although that still remains a goal, the new policy is designed to increase literacy levels, job readiness, and levels of income. These newer emphases are driven by a concern with the social costs of failed drug policies, especially the loss of African Americans and other people of color to the criminal justice system.

Broward County Dedicated Drug Treatment Court

The Miami and Oakland drug courts were diversionary in nature. Prosecution was withheld pending successful completion of treatment; then, charges were dismissed. The chapter in this volume by W. Clinton Terry, "Broward County's Dedicated Drug Treatment Court: From Postadjudication to Diversion," discusses the first of two postadjudication courts presented in this volume. Under a postadjudication model, defendants plead guilty or no contest to the drug charges filed against them and are sentenced to probation, a condition of which is participation in drug treatment. Successful completion of the treatment program results in a reduction of the length of probation to be served. The Broward County's Dedicated Drug Treatment Court, located in Fort Lauderdale, Florida, held out the promise to offenders who successfully completed treatment that their records could be expunged if they petitioned the court.

The first defendants entered Broward's dedicated drug treatment court in July 1991. The development of this court was strongly influenced by developments in Miami. Not only did local newspapers carry stories about Miami's drug court, which was only 20 to 30 miles from Fort Lauderdale, Florida, it was an easy trip to Miami to observe Miami's drug court and to meet and discuss issues with Judge Klein and other drug court participants. Interestingly, the use of contingency contracts and graduated sanctions—pioneered in Oakland—was recognized but not adopted by the planners of Broward's drug court.

The key problems confronting Broward during the late 1980s and early 1990s were virtually identical to those confronting Miami—increased use of cocaine, especially crack cocaine, jail overcrowding, and a concern for public safety.

Although many favored the adoption of a diversionary drug court model, the State Attorney favored a postadjudication model. Nevertheless, support for a diversionary drug court continued, and on October 1, 1993, just 2 years after beginning operations, Broward's dedicated drug treatment court became a diversionary court as a result of state legislative changes.

The assessment of Broward's dedicated drug treatment court compares drug court graduates with a group of randomly selected individuals who had also been arrested for the possession or purchase of cocaine and who were eligible for participation in the drug court but declined to participate. The data show that treatment graduates were statistically less likely to be rearrested for felony offenses than those released on probation and, perhaps more important, they were less likely to be rearrested for a drug offense. During the first year of the drug court, 39% of the people admitted to the program graduated.

The Portland Drug Court

As with the other early drug courts, Portland's first drug court resulted from increased drug arrests and prosecutions, after several years of dealing with crowded courtroom dockets. This is reported by Steve Belenko in his contribution, "Diverting Drug Offenders to Treatment Courts: The Portland Experience." Located in Multnomah County, Oregon, Portland's drug court, made use of available resources and was influenced by the personalities of the most active planners, most notably Judge Harl Haas, Portland's first drug court judge. Unlike the Miami, Oakland, and Broward County drug courts, however, Portland's court had a stronger history of funded substance abuse interventions, largely through the efforts of the Multnomah County Department of Corrections. These early efforts helped bring together different public and private agencies in an effort to deal with community substance abuse problems, thus helping establish a positive attitude toward the efficacy of treatment.

Portland accepted its first drug court client in August 1991. The drug court was known as STOP (Sanctions, Treatment, Opportunity, Progress), which was originally a treatment track of the county's planned expedited drug case management program funded by the Bureau of Justice Assistance. At the outset of planning, a number of individuals attended a treatment drug court workshop held by the National Judicial College. Later, they visited Miami's drug court. The planners liked what they saw in Miami and used it as a model for Portland's drug court.

As with the Miami and Oakland drug courts, the STOP program was a diversion program and operated as a partnership among the circuit court, district attorney, public defender, the Department of Community Corrections, and a contracted private treatment provider. Other groups and agencies also provided input. The STOP program lasted 12 months. If a person failed the program, there was a stipulated trial based only on the facts contained in the police report. The trials were scheduled during regular status hearings so that drug court participants could witness the consequences of failing the program.

The only data available measuring the impact of Portland's drug court compares clients who successfully completed the program with clients who failed to complete the program. The recidivism rates for program graduates were considerably lower than for those terminated from it.

Maricopa County Drug Court

The Maricopa County drug court, located in Phoenix, Arizona, began operations in March 1992. It was known as the FTDO (First Time Drug Offender) program. Like the Broward County Drug Court, it was developed as a postadjudication court. However, unlike Broward's drug court, which was strongly shaped by the State Attorney's public safety concerns, FTDO was shaped by the needs of the Maricopa County Adult Probation Department (MCAP), as described by Elizabeth Piper Deschenes and Rebecca D. Petersen in their contribution to this volume, "Experimenting with the Drug Court Model: Implementation and Change in Maricopa County, Arizona."

In considering how best to deal with their increasing population of drug-offending probationers, the MCAP was primarily concerned with developing a system of supervision and sanctions that would reduce drug use and recidivism. MCAP staff, along with two superior court judges and representatives from the county attorney's and public defender's offices, examined the drug courts in Miami and Oakland. They liked Oakland's FIRST program, with its contingency contracts and graduated sanctions as a means of providing clear levels of supervision, along with the promise of reducing periods of probation for those individuals able to complete their treatment in a timely fashion.

In Maricopa County, evaluation of the effectiveness of treatment, drug testing, and sanctions on offender behavior employed a true experimental design, randomly assigning individuals into four different groups. The evaluation revealed that more people received treatment in drug court, where it was mandatory, than during regular probation. About 41% had completed the treatment at the end of the study period, with an additional 18% still in treatment. In the 12-month period after they were sentenced to probation, there were no statistically significant differences in rearrests between the drug court group and the other groups on routine probation, nor was there any difference between the length of time it took for people to be rearrested. However, a lower proportion of drug court participants were sent to prison as a result of their rearrests. There was no reduction in overall substance abuse levels as measured by positive urine tests. The drug court participants were more likely to measure positive for marijuana, which was the second drug of choice behind alcohol, than those on regular probation. A second evaluation followed up 506 individuals from the original study group for a period of 36 months from date of sentencing. The long-term impact of drug court was a reduction in the arrest rate in comparison to those on routine probation. The drug court continues to be run by MCAP and has expanded significantly.

Drug Court Research

Surveying the literature on treatment drug courts, little is available that reveals much about the impact of treatment drug courts on the outcomes for which they were created. According to the most recent GAO (1997) examination of existing drug courts, the data "provide some limited information but do not permit firm conclusions regarding drug court impact" (p. 13). Do drug courts work? The jury is still out. Obviously, for the offenders who have benefited from participating in dedicated drug treatment courts, drug courts have been wonderful. For the treatment professionals and for court personnel, the success stories told at graduation ceremonies are heartwarming and soul-felt. However, a description of the larger picture remains to be written.

Most current reporting is limited to counting the number of people who graduate. Other examinations attempt to compare drug treatment graduates with other groups of individuals. The difficulty with many of these comparisons concerns the groups that are compared with one another. If for instance, the comparison is between program graduates and nongraduates, it is difficult to explain any differences that may appear because both groups were exposed to the treatment protocols. If the comparison is between dedicated drug treatment graduates and other groups of felony offenders, or between treatment graduates and other groups of substance abuse offenders who have been arrested but who have not received treatment, differences may be the result of prior criminal histories, the intensity of drug addiction, and readiness to receive treatment rather than the result of the treatment program.

Much needs to be accomplished within the area of dedicated drug treatment court research. At the top of the list is the use of experimental or quasi-experimental research designs. The former allows treatment participants to be randomly assigned to groups to minimize biases in group selection. If differences occur between groups when employing a random experimental design, these differences are most likely the result of program effects.

Quasi-experimental (comparison groups) are used frequently as a substitute for a random experimental design, when, for instance, treatment providers rule out the use of experimental designs for ethical reasons. In this case, groups are matched as closely as possible to one another to eliminate differences between groups. Unfortunately, to date, these relatively simple and well-understood research principles have not been widely employed in the research designs used to evaluate dedicated drug treatment courts.

Although use of experimental designs and/or comparison groups would represent a considerable improvement in the current level of treatment drug court research, interpreting their findings across the different jurisdictions within which they occur will be difficult. Different treatment courts are structured differently; admit differing types of individuals, perhaps with different drug use patterns; and expect different outcomes. Many treatment drug courts admit people into treatment who have prior felony histories, although most exclude people with histories of violence. Other programs admit only first-time drug offenders who have no prior criminal histories. The drug of choice found in some jurisdictions is marijuana, whereas in other areas, the drug of choice is powder and/or crack cocaine. Some treatment drug courts are postadjudication courts, whereas many others are diversion courts. The treatment programs provided by some drug courts contain minimal requirements, including low levels of supervision and drug testing; other programs have developed intensive outpatient programs involving numerous group and individual counseling sessions and frequent drug testing. With all of these differences, it will be difficult to compare findings.

Difficult may be good. It may be good because it forces analysts to search for both the commonalities and differences in programs to discover what works under what sorts of conditions. Nevertheless, as the number of dedicated drug treatment courts increases, their evaluation on a national basis becomes an increasingly difficult and complex task. This is discussed in John Goldkamp's last chapter of this volume, "Challenges for Research and Innovation: When Is a Drug Court Not a Drug Court?" Such a study is not impossible, but it would require some careful conceptual work delineating what is and what is not a drug court; the beginning of such a discussion is presented in Goldkamp's chapter.

Notes

1. These data were provided by a staff member of the National Association of Drug Court Professionals in March 1998, during a telephone conversation with the author.
2. Portions of this section have previously appeared in W. Clinton Terry III (1996), "Dedicated Drug Treatment Courts: A Collaborative Model of Justice for Local Government." Copyright 1996 The Council of State Governments. Reprinted with permission of *Spectrum: The Journal of State Government.*

References

Ashman, A. (1975). *Courts of limited jurisdiction: A national survey.* Chicago: American Judicature Society.

Baar, C. (1993). Trial court unification in practice. *Judicature, 76,* 179-184.

Belenko, S., & Dumanovsky, T. (1993). *Specialized drug courts: Program brief.* Washington, DC: U.S. Department of Justice, Bureau of Justice Assistance.

Berkson, L., & Carbon, S. (1978). *Court unification: History, politics, and implementation.* Washington, DC: National Institute of Law Enforcement and Criminal Justice.

Church, T. (1985). Examining local legal culture. *American Bar Foundation Research Journal, 1980,* 449-518.

Cooper, C. S., & Trotter, J. A., Jr. (1994a). *Drug case management and treatment intervention strategies in the state and local courts* (Vol. 1, rev.). Washington, DC: American University Press.

Cooper, C. S., & Trotter, J. A., Jr. (1994b) Recent developments in drug case management: Reengineering the judicial process. *The Justice System Journal, 17*(1), 83-98.

Falco, M. (1994). *The making of a drug-free America: Programs that work.* New York: Times Books.

Fleming, R., Nardulli, P., & Eisenstein, J. (1992). *The craft of justice: Politics and work in criminal court communities.* Philadelphia: University of Pennsylvania Press.

Gallas, G. (1979). Court reform: Has it been built on an adequate foundation. *Judicature, 63,* 28-38.

General Accounting Office (GAO). (1995). *Drug courts: Information on a new approach to address drug-related crime.* Washington, DC: Author.

General Accounting Office (GAO). (1997). *Drug courts: Overview of growth, characteristics, and results* (Report to the Committee on the Judiciary, U.S. Senate, and the Committee on the Judiciary, House of Representatives). Washington, DC: Government Printing Office.

Goerdt, J. A., Lomvardias, C., & Gallas, G. (1990). *Reexamining the pace of litigation in urban trial courts.* Williamsburg, VA: National Center for State Courts.

Goerdt, J. A., & Martin, J. A. (1989). The impact of drug cases on case processing in urban trial courts. *State Court Journal, 13*(4). 4-12.

Goldkamp, J. S. (1994). *Justice and treatment innovation: The drug court movement* (a working paper of the First National Drug Court Conference, December 1993). Washington, DC: U.S. Department of Justice, Office of Justice programs, National Institute of Justice.

Goldkamp, J. S., & Weiland, D. (1993). *Assessing the impact of Dade County's felony drug court: Final report.* Washington, DC: U.S. Department of Justice, Office of Justice Programs, National Institute of Justice.

Hudzik, J. (1985). Rethinking the consequences of state financing. *The Justice System Journal, 10*(985), 135-158.

Inciardi, J. A., McBride, D. C., & Rivers, J. E. (1996). *Drug control and the courts.* Thousand Oaks, CA: Sage.

Jacobs, H. (1991). Decision makers in trial courts. In J. Gates & C. Johnson (Eds.), *In the American courts: A critical assessment* (pp. 211-213). Washington, DC: CQ Press.

Lamber, J., & Luskin, M. L. (1992). Court reform: A view from the bottom. *Judicature, 75,* 295-299.

National Center for State Courts. (1996). *Oakland drug court assessment.* Denver, CO: Author.

National Institute of Justice. (1984). *The significance of judicial structure: The effect of unification on trial court operations.* Washington, DC: Author.

Neubauer, D. W. (1996). *America's courts and the criminal justice system.* Belmont, CA: Wadsworth.

Office of National Drug Control Policy. (1996). *The national drug control strategy: 1996.* Washington, DC: Author.

President's Commission on Law Enforcement and the Administration of Justice. (1967). *The courts* (Task force report). Washington, DC: Government Printing Office.

Provine, D. M., & Seron, C.. (1995). Innovation and reform in courts: A cross-cultural perspective. In G. L. Mays & P. R. Gregware (Eds.), *In courts and justice: A reader.* Prospect Heights, IL: Waveland Press.

Rubin, T. (1984). *The courts: Fulcrum of the justice system* (2nd ed.). New York: Random House.

Smith, B. E., Davis, R., & Goretsky, S. (1991). *Strategies for courts to cope with the caseload pressures of drug cases: Final report.* Chicago: American Bar Association.

Smith, B. E., Davis, R. C., & Lurigio, A. J. (1994). Introduction to the special issue. *The Justice System Journal, 17*(1), pp. v-x.

Stout, R. (1986). Planning for unified court budgeting. *Judicature, 69*(4), 205-213.

Substance Abuse and Mental Health Services Administration. (1996). *Preliminary estimates from the 1995 National Household Survey on Drug Abuse.* Washington, DC: Author.

Tarr, G. A. (1981). Court unification and court performance: A preliminary assessment. *Judicature, 64*(8), 356-368.

Terry, W. C., III. (1996). Dedicated drug treatment courts: A collaborative model of justice for local government. *Spectrum: The Journal of State Government, 69*(3), 37-48.

U.S. Department of Justice, Federal Bureau of Investigation. (1990). *Uniform crime reports for the United States, 1989.* Washington, DC: Government Printing Office.

Wice, P. B. (1985). *Chaos in the courthouse: Inner workings of urban criminal courts.* Westport, CT: Praeger.

2. The Origin of the Treatment Drug Court in Miami

John S. Goldkamp

In 1999, there is a sizable and increasingly accepted movement across the country to establish drug courts. In the summer of 1989, Dade County (Miami) courts became the pioneer in this development when the first treatment drug court was opened there. The Dade County innovation, which still operates today at the ripe old age of 10, represented an extraordinary and, at the time, unique local effort to deal with drug-related crime and its impact. One could argue that Dade County, with its diverse population and collection of municipalities sitting at the gateway to the Caribbean and Latin America and with its special challenges (such as waves of refugees from Cuba and Haiti), provided a highly unusual setting for the drug

AUTHOR'S NOTE: Portions of this chapter were adapted from Goldkamp, 1994b, p. 110.

court experiment. The speed with which the Miami Drug Court Model has spread to jurisdictions nationwide confirms that, its special attributes as a setting notwithstanding, the challenges facing Miami were not unique. In fact, they were shared by many American jurisdictions, large and small, during the period of the so-called War on Drugs. A variety of sources have documented the growth and impact of the drug-related criminal caseload in many jurisdictions across the United States during the 1980s (Belenko, 1990; Goerdt, Lomvadias, Gallas, & Mahoney, 1989; Goerdt & Martin, 1989; Goldkamp et al., 1990b).[1] The increases in arrests for drug violations nationally, coinciding with a dramatic increase in the availability and use of cocaine and, later, crack cocaine, translated into burgeoning criminal caseloads in the courts of most urban centers. Depending on one's definition—particularly when moving beyond the basic category of people charged with drug crimes—the majority of criminal cases entering criminal processing could at that time (and arguably still) be classified as drug-related (Goldkamp et al., 1990a). The impact of the drug caseload of the late 1980s posed serious challenges for most criminal justice agencies, including police, prosecutors, defense systems, jails, prisons, and probation and parole agencies. Particularly in Dade County, the burgeoning drug-related caseload exacerbated already difficult problems of correctional overcrowding and court backlogs, sparking public safety concerns about drug-crime violence and raising questions among the public about the effectiveness of the justice system.

Toward the end of the 1980s, however, there were signs that punitive approaches to substance abuse problems both (a) could not be indefinitely sustained by increasing uses of imprisonment and (b) did not appear to deliver expected results in reducing drug abuse and related crime. In its 1993 report, the Criminal Justice Section of the American Bar Association (ABA) argued, for example, that the recent focus of law enforcement and confinement resources on drug offenders was not only ineffective but also occurred at the expense of dealing with violent crime and other serious offenses. This theme was later also strongly argued by Janet Reno, formerly Dade County State Attorney, then Attorney General of the United States, who questioned the impact of mandatory minimum sentences for drug offenders and advocated development of initiatives focusing on preventing crime and providing alternatives to punitive imprisonment.

Before the "re-discovery" of the drug treatment response in Miami, urban court systems were compelled to develop strategies to cope with the problem of huge increases in drug-related cases. In an ABA study describing the responses of court systems, Smith, Davis, and Goretsky (1991) identified three kinds of judicial strategies, including strategies focusing on case processing management, development of specialized courts or approaches to drug cases (the first drug courts), and on "sentencing or diversionary alternatives" (p. 7). In their review of these approaches, Smith et al. described the Philadelphia Court of Common Pleas as an example of a court system implementing an overall case-flow management strategy, Cook County Circuit Court's Night Court and Milwaukee Circuit Court's Speedy Trial Project as examples of specialized approaches to drug cases, and Dade County Circuit Court's drug court as an example of sentencing or diversionary alternatives to the drug-caseload glut. Invented as a response to the extreme pressures of the drug caseload of the 1980s, Dade County's felony drug court does fall comfortably under the diversionary category outlined by Smith et al. (1991). Certainly, the Miami Drug Court Model—as that court and its treatment strategy have come to be known—builds on a fundamental diversionary emphasis in its operation. Yet, *diversion,* as it is popularly understood,[2] does not fully convey the substance and character of the Miami innovation. Although it just as certainly had important implications for case-flow management and specialization in criminal courts, its main contribution was as an alternative processing system in which justice and treatment innovation would be intertwined for better results, but not without some considerable effort.

In Dade County, during the entire decade of the 1980s, the numbers of reported crimes and adult arrests had risen steadily. Adult arrests had increased about 45% between 1985 and 1989 alone, while arrests for drug possession had increased 93% during that 5-year interval (Goldkamp & Weiland, 1991). Misdemeanor and felony filings more than doubled from 1978 to 1990. Dispositions of felonies in Circuit Court nearly kept up with filings until 1989, when, as the increase in felony filings continued uninterrupted, the number of dispositions began to decline. The number of felony cases pending at the end of the year had increased three and one-half times from 1979 to 1990. The rapid geometric growth of the drug caseload came at a time when Dade County's correctional facilities were in their second decade of a long-standing overcrowding crisis, with litigation in Federal Court still ongoing. The pervasive impact of drug-involved offenders on the criminal caseload in Dade County was illustrated by a study of 1987 felony defendants (Goldkamp,

Gottfredson, and Weiland, 1990; Goldkamp, Jones, Gottfredson, and Weiland, 1990a, 1990b), which found that about 73% of entering felony defendants tested positively for cocaine and that at least 83% could in some way be classified as drug-related (that is, they tested positively for drugs, were charged with drug offenses, and/or had prior records of drug offenses).

In a most basic sense, the implementation of the Miami Drug Court in 1989 was a response to this extraordinary growth in the drug-related criminal caseload in Dade County, to the strain it placed on most aspects of the criminal justice system, and to the perceived impact of drug-related crime and criminals on public safety in Dade County. Just as certainly, the court innovation grew out of a shared sense of futility and desperation among criminal justice leaders that "normal" emergency measures were not having the desired impact. The various Dade County police agencies were devoting more resources to investigation of drug crimes and generating more arrests, increasing the volume of cases awaiting processing by the courts. Yet, the availability of drugs, particularly cocaine and crack cocaine, seemed unrelenting, given Dade County's location at the gateway to drug-trafficking routes north from Central and Latin America. As quickly as the State Attorney could prosecute, the cases kept coming, and the overcrowded jails and prisons had to release offenders at a rapid pace. As the judicial leaders, the State Attorney, and the Chief Public Defender sought to make the system work under the strain, it seemed that more cases were being processed faster, jail and prison cells were being filled, and probation and pretrial services were being overwhelmed, all with little apparent impact on the problem.

The Chief Judge, the Honorable Gerald T. Wetherington, assigned the Honorable Herbert Klein, one of his most respected judges, to investigate options to respond to the crisis posed by the drug-related criminal caseload. With the strong support and leadership of the prosecutor, the result was a carefully crafted and dramatically new court-centered program, emphasizing drug treatment, responsibility, and accountability (or offering, as Janet Reno would often explain, "both a carrot and a stick"). After careful critique, discussion, and modification, the proposed drug court program won the support of the Public Defender, who was critically concerned about the due process (and other) rights of defendants affected by participation in the program and about the potential onerousness of the proposed 12-month treatment approach. (They noted that 12 months of intensive treatment and frequent reporting in person to a judge were likely to be seen as much more demanding by many offenders than a few months in jail and/or on probation, the usual disposition in eligible cases.)

In retrospect, it is difficult to appreciate how dramatically the proposed drug court in Miami cut against the grain of national drug and crime policy at the time and departed from accepted norms within the judiciary in the United States. It is an understatement to report that the Bush administration was not emphasizing drug treatment in its national drug control strategy for demand reduction at the end of the 1980s, but rather favored policies emphasizing punishment and deterrence (see The White House, 1989). No federal funds were made available to assist the local drug court enterprise. In fact, a direct request for financial support for the Miami Drug Court to then-drug czar William Bennett was rebuffed with little discussion and little interest shown. The reaction was not much more sympathetic within the national judicial community.

At a 1989 meeting of the "Big Nine" court systems, convened to discuss the drug caseload problem posed for the nation's largest courts, high-ranking court officials in the nine most populous jurisdictions spoke about court strategies that would process drug cases more quickly and coolly ignored suggestions to develop court-based treatment approaches. Alone at that Philadelphia meeting, Judge Klein from Miami argued that the answer was not to be found in making the machinery of justice spin faster, but rather in developing an effective strategy of court-supervised drug treatment in a way that had never before been attempted in the criminal courts. This author witnessed the reaction of the distinguished judicial leaders at that meeting to Judge Klein's drug court proposition, emphasizing the concepts of treatment and rehabilitation. His proposal was met with what can best be described as embarrassed silence and out-of-hand dismissal of ideas that were viewed as behind the times. The other judicial leaders believed that Judge Klein was an idealist and that his approach could contribute little to practical solution of the drug-involved caseload problems the conference was convened to discuss.[3]

In assembling the key elements of what was to become the Miami Drug Court, the Dade County judicial leaders, State Attorney, and Public Defender unwittingly paved the way for the national drug court movement, which, since its start in Miami in 1989, has grown to include courts in possibly hundreds of American jurisdictions. This chapter describes some of the key ingredients of the original

Miami Drug Court Model and discusses findings from an evaluation[4] conducted in the court's early stages of implementation. Examination of the pioneering efforts in Dade County is important not only in assessing the Miami prototype, but also because it represented a first step in identifying issues for research to address and set the stage for surveying the now much larger movement toward establishing treatment drug courts in the United States.

The Elements of Dade County's Felony Drug Court: The Miami Model

The combination of two principal components—the role of officials in the courtroom and the operation of a specially adapted program of primarily outpatient[5] drug abuse treatment—formed the basis of what has come to be known as the Miami Drug Court Model. Although other diversion approaches in the United States over the last couple of decades have undoubtedly referred defendants to drug abuse treatment programs, it is the courtroom-based team approach to treatment—and particularly the central, hands-on judicial role—that has distinguished Dade County's approach from other previous court initiatives aiming at the drug-related caseload.

The Drug Court Courtroom

The courtroom component of the Miami felony drug court has been described by Dade County's Executive Assistant Public Defender David Weed as a "theater in the square," because it departs from the normal, adversarial criminal courtroom mode of operation in several respects. First, and most significant, is the role of the drug court judge. In the Miami model, the judge presides over many brief hearings in which he or she engages in conversation directly with the defendant/participant, without the intervening or translating role of counsel as mouthpiece. The judge-to-defendant exchanges may involve a defendant's entry into the program, in-court reports on a defendant's progress, graduation of defendants from the program, or a variety of sanctioning decisions involving defendants who have absconded or been rearrested for new offenses. Defendants who have opted to enter the program are instructed by the judge to appear in court periodically for reviews of their progress in treatment. On the basis of input from the treatment agency—referred to as the DATP (Diversion and Treatment Program)[6]—the judge hears reports of the defendant's progress, discusses his/her status in treatment with the defendant, and offers encouragement if appropriate. Often, the judge listens to a defendant's explanation of why he or she didn't comply with required attendance, then encourages the defendant to get back into treatment. The judge, who can be encouraging and supportive, is also called on to impose sanctions or otherwise encourage compliance with program requirements when the defendant has shown a poor record of performance, or, for example, is rearrested and is brought back to the drug court on an alias capias (felony bench warrant). On occasion, the judge will order the defendant confined for 2 weeks in jail ("motivational jail"), in an area reserved for drug court defendants to receive jail-based treatment, and will reassess the defendant's participation after that period of confinement. The judge also may transfer the cases of some defendants out of drug court to be tried in the normal fashion by other Circuit Court felony judges.

The unusual role of the judge, however, is best understood in the context of the unorthodox, nonadversarial, and team-oriented roles played by the other criminal justice officials in the courtroom, roles designed to support the judge's role and to contribute to the treatment progress of the drug-involved felony defendants coming through the court. The priority given to defendants' treatment progress and transactions in the courtroom seem, at times, more like psychodrama or therapeutic community treatment modalities than normal criminal courtroom proceedings. Most noticeable are the transformed roles of the prosecutor and defender. The prosecutor in the courtroom shifts between communicating strong encouragement for defendants who appear to be making progress to raising the prospects of reinstating formal prosecution of charges when defendants do not seem to be participating appropriately in treatment. The defender seems clearly supportive of the opportunity drug court provides and also plays a role that appears more therapeutic in nature than adversarial. Representatives of the treatment program and Pretrial Services attend the hearings, so that the judge is kept up-to-date on developments in each case.

The Drug Court's Treatment Program

Since the drug court first opened in 1989, defendants have been referred primarily to the county-run DATP, an outpatient program tailored for the drug court with centers eventually in four locations in Dade County. There was also an option for defendants who lived in other jurisdictions to participate in treatment programs outside of Dade County, as long as regular reports were made to the court regarding their progress. The drug court was initially designed to accept defendants who were charged with third-degree felony drug-possession offenses and who had no prior convictions. The rationale for these eligibility criteria was that, although the Circuit Court wanted to target felony defendants, it did not want to begin with defendants who posed serious risks to public safety. In addition, it was reasoned that, over the long run, the greatest payoff would come from investing treatment and court resources in defendants with drug problems who were at the beginning of their criminal involvement (had no prior criminal histories), thereby increasing the likelihood of preventing their further involvement. Over time, however, defendants with prior convictions have also been admitted to the court.

The DATP treatment program was designed to require 1 year's participation by drug-involved felony defendants, during which the defendants would proceed from nonmedical detoxification (Phase I), to counseling (Phase II), to educational/vocational assessment and training (Phase III), and then to graduation. Phase I was intended to require a minimum of 12 consecutive days of clinic visits or as many days as were required to achieve seven consecutive negative urine tests. In Phase II, the number of required visits was generally reduced to three or even two per week, with a urine test at each visit. During Phase III, attendance requirements might continue to be the same or be relaxed somewhat, given a client's progress and work schedule or school obligations. At any time, three consecutive unauthorized failures to keep required clinic appointments would result in the client's placement in Phase V. A client returning after such an absence would be reinstated in whatever phase he or she had been in. If a client failed to appear for 30 consecutive days, in compliance with state regulations, DATP was required to close that client's file. Although clients were commonly readmitted even after such an extended absence, they would be required to start over in Phase I. Acupuncture and drug testing were incorporated into the treatment regime as tools to support the treatment process, but they were not considered treatment modalities in themselves. (In fact, acupuncture was and is undertaken on a voluntarily basis by program participants.) Recognizing that drug-abusing offenders are a group with a number of related problem behaviors, it was anticipated that the time spent in Phase I or Phase II of the program might vary notably for different defendants and that setbacks would probably occur. The difficulty of dealing with drug-involved defendants notwithstanding, the aims of the program included reduction of drug abuse and of drug abuse-related criminal behavior among participating defendants over the length of the program and, it was hoped, subsequent to it.

Marrying Drug Treatment Methods and Criminal Justice Goals: The Major Challenge of the Miami Drug Court Model

With no similar program already in existence on which to model the Miami Drug Court, the treatment drug court model designed in Florida's Eleventh Circuit was formed as a hybrid, combining elements of criminal justice and drug treatment approaches to address an important portion of the drug-involved criminal justice population. Key elements included the special role for the judge and criminal courtroom personnel, the fundamental treatment orientation, and the diversion-like framework. This attempt to integrate disparate elements meant trying to join two perspectives accustomed to different methods and sometimes competing aims regarding drug involvement and its reduction. The adaptation of the courtroom setting and procedures to complement the more flexible aims of treatment, for example, raised conflicts with the normally more formal and adversarial criminal justice aims and procedures. The drug court judge, the State Attorney, and the Public Defender all would assume that drug-involved defendants, by definition, are likely to have a difficult time in the treatment process and, in fact, may at first fail repeatedly.

This expectation of failure and the necessity for program flexibility were then and still are antithetical to the standard criminal justice perspective, which would first seek to adjudicate criminal charges and impose punishment and then seek to sanction deviations from conditions of provisional liberty that had been imposed, through revocation of release or, at least, imposition of more restrictive conditions. One could easily imagine that an approach based on a more conventional application of fixed graduated sanctions for enforcing compliance with program conditions might have the effect of backfiring by identifying drug-involved defendants who ordinarily would not have been identified and then invoking sanctions when conditions were quickly breached. To the extent that incarceration would be employed as an enforcement sanction, as is currently the case with a handful of newer drug courts, an inflexible approach to achieving program compliance might then result in an increase in jailing, as opposed to the reduction assumed by the program.

The drug treatment program that was designed to serve the Miami Drug Court has had to accommodate criminal justice concerns that ordinarily would not have been given such weight by a treatment agency. For example, a clear goal of the drug court was to provide defendants with the opportunity to undergo drug treatment in the hope that reduced drug abuse would translate into reduced criminal behavior. In the hope that reduced participation in criminal behavior in the near term would translate into a smaller returning criminal caseload in the future, an assumption of the drug court approach is that investment now in drug treatment of felony defendants will contribute to reduced criminal caseload strain later. However, reduction in drug abuse among drug court defendants, by itself—the standard primary aim of drug abuse treatment programs—would not satisfy the goals of the drug court. The production of more drug-free criminals would not be considered an acceptable outcome of the drug court, although it might be viewed as a favorable outcome from a drug treatment perspective alone.

Another example of conflicting aims and methods is found in the area of determining when a client could or should be terminated from drug treatment for failing to demonstrate sufficient participation in the process. Ordinarily, the drug treatment program itself would choose to exercise the authority to terminate a defendant from treatment when it was determined to be appropriate. Under the Dade County approach, however, it is the judge who decides whether a defendant should be terminated from treatment and the judge who, in practice, sends defendants back to treatment without the prior approval of the treatment staff itself. In fact, officials report that it is very hard for a defendant to be rejected from treatment once the drug court process has begun. On the other hand, no matter how well a defendant has been doing in early stages of treatment, rearrest for a more serious crime will result in transfer to the normal adjudication process.

The specially negotiated working relationship between drug treatment methods and criminal justice goals at the core of the Miami Drug Court Model may represent the most important challenge underlying implementation and operation of such a court. It also raises a particular challenge for evaluation research and complicates design of an empirical assessment. Because organization of an appropriate research design must begin with a clear understanding of what the drug court is trying to accomplish—its announced goals—

it is essential to make explicit some of the implications of the dual perspective. In a sense, the major challenge of the drug court is to try to bring treatment to large numbers of offenders in a system in which this approach has, until recently, been inconceivable.

Illustrating the Competing Perspectives

Figure 2.1 illustrates some of the implications of the goals, methods, and outcome measures associated with the two perspectives for designing an assessment of the drug court. Seen from the vantage point of drug abuse treatment, the goals of the drug court would primarily center on reducing drug abuse and related behavior so that client-defendants could function more normally in society. From the perspective of the criminal justice system, the aims of the drug court program would more likely include reducing the impact of the drug caseload on case-processing resources (by diverting the flow of cases and reducing the future caseload), reducing drug crime among participants, and, thereby, improving public safety.

The drug treatment perspective would make use of a variety of methods and program options to bring about its goal of reduced drug abuse behavior among its clients, beginning with an initial assessment of the client's drug problem, an initial detoxification phase, the use of approaches to improve the clients' ability to receive treatment (such as maintenance or acupuncture programs), the use of various treatment modalities as appropriate (often involving counseling and group techniques), placement in outpatient (community-based) or inpatient (residential) settings, and the integration of other life skills improvement strategies (such as educational or vocational training programs). The criminal justice perspective would conceive of the drug court principally as a diversion program and would see its responsibility as involving referral of defendants to drug treatment options operated outside of the criminal justice system. The role of the drug court would be to approve such referrals (presumably at the recommendation of the prosecutor), to order appropriate monitoring or supervision of the defendants in diversion status, and to enforce the conditions of diversion appropriately, including revocation of diversionary status, revocation of preadjudicatory release, and scheduling of cases for adjudication in the normal fashion.

The drug treatment and criminal justice perspectives might also define the target populations most appropriate for drug court processing quite differently. Several criteria would be central in the

Perspective	*Goals*	*Methods/Options*	*ID Target Population*	*Expectations of Performance*	*Measures of Effectiveness (Outcomes)*
Drug Treatment	• Reducing drug abuse and associated behavior	• ID/diagnose • Detoxification • Maintenance • Acupuncture • Various treatments • (counseling) • Outpatient/Inpatient • Educational-vocational training	• Occasional/regular/daily user/treaters • Type of drug • Beginning/advanced (addict) • Younger/older	• Counselors • Access to community based on treatment needs • Expect failure and slow progress • Flexibility and adjustment	• Reduced abuse • Abstinence • Increased performance • Improved skills • Improved health
Criminal Justice	• Reduced impact of drug caseload (divert flow, reduce future caseload return) • Reduced crowding • Curb drug crime among participants • Improve public safety generally	• Diversion/referral • Sanctions to enforce release conditions • Informal versus formal processing • Monitoring/supervision • Incarceration	• Charge/priors • Less serious/lower risk to public safety • Serious enough not to "widen net" (not misdemeanors) • Self-report/drug test • "Jail-bound" or not	• Formal roles (judges, probation, prosecution, defense, etc.) • Probation-like supervision or monitoring • Enforcement of conditions of provisional liberty • Sanctions for failure including revocation, incarceration	• Reduced current/future caseload • Abstinence • Reduced crime

Figure 2.1. Drug Treatment and Criminal Justice Goals, Methods, and Outcomes

identification of the target population from the drug treatment perspective. Potential clients would be classified according to the nature of their drug abuse problems, including the type(s) of substances abused (cocaine, heroin, barbiturates, benzodiazepines, hallucinogens, alcohol, polydrug, or other types of abuse substances), the reported frequency of use (e.g., occasional, regular, daily), and the method of abuse (intravenous, oral, inhaling, smoking, etc.). Part of the initial classification of abusers by treatment staff might also consider the stage of the abuse career (whether the client is at the beginning or more advanced stages of drug involvement) and the relative ability (or inability) of the defendant to function normally. The age of the drug abuser might, therefore, also figure into the targeting of drug abusers for the drug court treatment program. Classification of candidate drug abusers according to these kinds of criteria would result in the identification of treatment-relevant abuse categories that could target individuals for different treatment approaches.

A criminal justice approach to targeting defendants for drug court involvement would be likely to focus on other kinds of eligibility criteria, beginning with the types of criminal charges involved in the instant arrest and the patterns of prior convictions. An aim of such an approach would be to identify categories of defendants with drug-related cases (hence, the presence of drug charges) and prior criminal histories that would suggest their candidacy in the drug court program would not pose undue risk to the public safety. The criminal justice perspective would likely target defendants with cases that were serious enough to involve a suitably challenging category of drug-involved defendants (so that net-widening could be avoided and possibly some pretrial and postconviction incarceration eliminated), yet, not so serious as to be seen as inappropriately demeaning the seriousness of criminal offenses or risking public safety. If correctional crowding were severe, the criminal justice approach might focus on defendants who were clearly jail bound, so that jail population pressures could be reduced.

Given the competing expectable approaches to defining eligibility for the program, it is notable that the actual approach—focusing on felony defendants with drug possession and related charges—makes use of elements of both perspectives. From the criminal justice point of view, a reasonable category of defendants likely to have drug abuse problems is identified by aiming at third-degree felony drug possession cases (assuming that drug possession will often indicate drug use). From a drug abuse treatment perspective, this approach singles out drug abusers who have not yet progressed into serious criminal involvement, providing the opportunity to avoid the amplification of criminal activity that is thought to accompany more serious drug involvement. Reliance on criminal charges also serves as a simpler and much less costly approach to identification of drug abusers than arrest-stage drug testing and perhaps a more reliable means than defendant self-reports drawn from the pretrial services interview.

Perhaps, the difference between the two perspectives is most sharply illustrated in the expectations of performance of drug-involved defendants in the drug court program. It is likely that the criminal justice perspective would set forth conditions that the defendant would agree to and then expect those conditions to be met. In the event of noncompliance, defendants would risk being dropped from the program and made subject to adjudication of their charges in a normal setting—and, quite likely, they would experience pretrial detention in the interim. In contrast, a treatment perspective would probably not view a "three strikes" approach to program compliance as realistic. Indeed, treatment staff would understand that, to the extent that serious drug abusers are encouraged to enter the program, the road to progress is likely to be very difficult, with initial failures to be expected.

This difference in expectations about the performance of the participating drug-involved defendants translates into differences in approaches to measuring outcomes in an assessment. If it is a reasonable assumption that progress in drug treatment will be, by definition, very difficult at times, then the measure of outcomes probably would not focus on all of the interim missteps, but rather on ultimate reduction of drug abuse, eventual abstinence, and improvement of life skills. The criminal justice perspective would insist on abstinence as a goal and would be certain to measure reinvolvement in crime during and after treatment as important outcomes. Clearly, production of drug-free and healthy repeating criminals would not be an outcome likely to be acceptable from the criminal justice perspective. The contrasting perspectives of the two worldviews, from the different viewpoints of drug treatment and criminal court processing, form the tensions in the conceptual foundation of the treatment drug court model and set the requirements for a sufficiently open evaluative approach.

Findings From Evaluation Research

At the request of the court leadership, we carried out an evaluation of the Miami Drug Court in its early phase of implementation, following cases entering the court in August and September of 1990 over an 18-month period. The aims of the research included investigation of (a) the impact of drug court on criminal case processing, including the selection and enrollment of felony defendants who would have been adjudicated in the normal fashion; (b) comparison of the case outcomes of drug court defendants with the outcomes of defendants charged with offenses of similar severity, both prior to the inception of drug court and contemporaneous to the processing of drug court defendants; (c) the performance of drug court defendants participating in the treatment program, including treatment program outcomes; and (d) the public safety implications of the drug court program, particularly when compared to other categories of Dade County felony defendants. The basic aim of the multisample study[7] was to identify the relative strengths and weaknesses of the drug court approach, to provide feedback to the Circuit Court and local officials to consider in further refinement of the program, and to share findings about its impact with other interested American jurisdictions.[8]

Given the unusual and ambitious agenda set by the Dade County drug court, the evaluation was designed to examine questions about its impact on defendants and on the criminal caseload. Basically, this was done empirically by studying the participation of drug court defendants in the treatment process and by comparing their case outcomes and criminal reinvolvement over an 18-month observation period with the outcomes associated with contemporaneous samples of felony defendants and samples of felony defendants entering Circuit Court during a period prior to the establishment of drug court. The findings, which are discussed in detail elsewhere, are summarized briefly here (see Goldkamp & Weiland, 1993a, 1993b, 1993c).

The Scope of the Drug Court Program

The Miami Drug Court has handled a large volume of cases of felony drug defendants since its inception. Indeed, it expanded its eligibility criteria somewhat over time and made other program improvements (such as adding the ability to refer a limited number of drug court defendants to residential placements as well as a short-term jail detoxification capacity). Second- as well as third-degree felony drug defendants have been admitted to the program, some directly at the initial stage of processing, some after being transferred from other courts. A minority of drug court defendants had prior arrests or convictions. Given that participation in the program was voluntary, it would be unlikely to expect 100% of potential candidates to enter the drug court. In fact, we estimated that roughly 83% of defendants identified as eligible and assigned to drug court actually entered treatment during the study period. This shows a reasonably effective enrollment or screening mechanism, which identified program candidates at the earliest stages of processing.[9]

Impact on the Criminal Caseload: Size of the Target Population

The drug court program initially targeted third-degree felony drug possession cases with no prior convictions. By the time of the 1990 sample employed in this study (about a year into the court's operation), people with initial charges involving selected second-degree drug felonies (purchase of drugs) were considered for the program, as well as some defendants with prior convictions. One way of estimating the impact of the program on the felony caseload, therefore, is to determine the proportion of relevant felony cases that would have been eligible for the program and the proportion actually entering the program. We began by estimating that about 39% of all entering second- and third-degree felony cases were cases involving drug offenses during the study period. About 13% of those cases were identified as eligible and scheduled for drug court. This amounted to about 5% of all entering second- and third-degree felony cases. Given that monthly admissions included some cases filed during previous months, monthly admissions to treatment through drug court were equivalent to about 7% of second- and third-degree felony filings during the months studied.

Impact on the Criminal Processing: Comparative Case Outcomes

We also tried to obtain an estimate of the impact of the drug court on the caseload by contrasting the outcomes of drug court defendants with the outcomes recorded by other types of felony defendants, as reflected by the comparison samples from 1990 and 1987. Drug court was planned on the assumption that defendants would at a minimum require about a year to complete the program successfully. Thus, we might project that these cases would be less quickly completed (adjudicated) than typical felony cases, and that when completed, they would more often show nolle prosequi or case-sealed outcomes.

Case outcomes of drug court defendants indeed differed sharply from those of other felony defendants. As expected, diversion types of outcomes (diverted, nolle prossed, case sealed) were much more frequently recorded for drug court defendants during the 18-month observation period. Another largely expected difference was that drug court cases took longer to complete; nearly one third of drug court cases were still open (unadjudicated) by the end of an 18-month observation period. In contrast, almost all other felony defendants had cases completed within that period of time. This finding, that the drug court caseload is not disposed of as promptly as other criminal cases of comparable seriousness,[10] is, in a sense, expected and mostly explained by two phenomena: Some defendants stay (are allowed to stay) in the treatment program for much longer than originally anticipated, and some defendants abscond from the program, thus leaving their cases in an indefinite active status. It is difficult to determine with certainty whether the longer completion time contributes to greater use of court resources than normal criminal processing does. However, an important question is whether the processing of drug court cases requires fewer or greater court resources than normal criminal adjudication, even though normal adjudication may occur more promptly.

Another apparent difference in the processing of drug court defendants is that slightly or dramatically greater proportions of the cases of the other felony defendants in 1990 and 1987 were dropped or dismissed (including "no action"). This raises the question of whether drug court processes some cases that, if processed through normal adjudicatory channels, might have been dropped from the system. From a treatment perspective, this may not be an important distinction. However, from a criminal justice perspective, this question takes on importance in several ways. First, from a net-widening perspective, drug court would be more efficient if it were to focus on cases most likely to be processed farther into the system. Thus, in addition to addressing the drug abuse treatment needs of the defendants, cases are diverted from criminal court processing and, in many cases, from correctional institutions—even if only temporarily. Finally, compared to other felony drug and nondrug defendants being processed contemporaneously, far fewer drug court defendants ended up with sentences to incarceration for terms of more than 1 year.

Treatment Program Performance

The early program outcomes were promising, particularly when compared to other results from other treatment programs.[11] Including all defendants (those with favorable and unfavorable outcomes) entering drug court during the sample period, the average (median) length of stay in the 1-year program was about 9 months. About one third of drug court defendants were continuing in the program after a 1-year period. Although some defendants moved forward through the successive program phases smoothly, nearly one third started over in Phase I at least once. In fact, about 7% of the admissions cohort were readmissions, or people who had been in the program previously. According to one version of measuring program success, excluding defendants whose criminal cases were dropped within the first month, or those who were not in the program for a sufficient start-up period (21 days), or defendants who were transferred to other jurisdictions, 60 percent of defendants could be classified as having favorable program outcomes.[12]

The Use of Short-Term Pretrial Detention to Support Program Participation: Motivational Jail

Dade County officials have argued that an important aspect of the drug court program is the judge's ability to make use of pretrial confinement when defendants are having great difficulty in participating adequately in the outpatient treatment approach of the DATP. As the program evolved, it became clear to the drug court judge, who had the prosecutor's support, that from time to time, some defendants would need to be removed from their environments for a short period to detoxify in a more structured environment. The use of a 2-week period of pretrial confinement was intended to provide an option between dismissing a defendant from the program (to face adjudication under normal procedures) and allowing him or her to flounder disastrously on the streets.

One of the concerns raised about such a practice was that, given the poor performance likely to be associated with heavily drug-involved defendants, short-term jailing would be overused and, in fact, could ultimately result in more confinement overall. Thus, in a jurisdiction having a history of jail crowding, there was concern not to exacerbate the crowding situation by exercising this program sanction. In addition, questions were raised about the possibility that the motivational jailing approach could end up jailing defendants who would not otherwise be jailed; that is, they would be confined only because of their drug dependence. After a full discussion of these issues, as a result of the drug court's need to pull in defendants having difficulty in attending the treatment program and appearing in court as required, a limited number of drug court beds were set aside in the Dade correctional facilities. According to statistics assembled by the Office of the State Attorney as of February 24, 1992, for example, about 37% of defendants entering the drug court program since its inception in 1989 (2,245 defendants) had experienced some motivational jail. According to the records of the State Attorney, about 18% of the sample defendants had been jailed at least once, 5% were jailed two times, and 5% were jailed three or more times.

Comparative Criminal Justice Outcomes: Rearrest and Failure to Attend Court

The criminal justice and public safety outcomes must be considered promising, at least in a comparative sense. At 32%, drug court defendants generated somewhat lower rates of reoffending (as indicated by rearrests) than 1990 nondrug felony defendants and notably lower rates of reoffending than 1990 other (non-drug court) second- and third-degree felony drug defendants. At the same time, when compared to felony drug defendants processed into Circuit Court in 1987, 2 years prior to implementation of the drug court, drug court defendants showed much lower rates of rearrest, even when controls were exercised for possible differences in sample composition. Perhaps the most striking finding is that when drug court defendants were rearrested, they averaged two to three times longer to first rearrest than all comparison group defendants. If generalizable to all drug court defendants since the time of this study—and there have been more than 4,000 admitted since the program began—these findings have important implications for the criminal caseload of Circuit Court. Not only did drug court defendants appear to reoffend less often, those who did reoffend delayed reoffending for considerable periods.[13]

Perhaps the most troublesome finding, however, is one that could have been predicted: As drug court defendants were required to appear in court periodically throughout their participation in treatment, the opportunity was provided to record failures-to-appear (FTAs) in court at a rate above that normally shown by Dade County felony defendants. (More than half of drug court defendants recorded FTAs in drug court at least once, compared to from 2% to 11% of other felony defendants.) These high rates of missed court hearings, however, are clearly an artifact of requiring so many more court hearings than would normally be the case in processing criminal charges. This phenomenon is similar to that experienced by many programs granting provisional liberty to defendants and offenders and suggests that approaches should be devised to monitor appearance more closely and to prevent such levels of defendant failure-to-appear.

Beyond the Miami Model of Treatment Drug Court

The original innovation of the treatment drug court in Miami is of interest not only because it sheds light on the developments of the specific program in the Miami courts, but also because it provides the threads of change that have been woven into successive generations of drug courts and spinoffs that represent significant departures from traditional court practices in the United States. The challenges faced in a first-ever effort at implementation, along with the research findings describing the impact of the early stages of the drug court experience in Miami, reflect an unusual kind of reform in the criminal courts: a reform that sought to find common ground between a strictly criminal justice processing approach and the methods and values of drug treatment. This multidisciplinary approach has been greatly expanded in the original Miami court, and it has also been amplified in many of the succeeding drug courts in other jurisdictions. Along the way, the Dade County leaders broke down some traditional barriers relating to the roles of the criminal court judge, of defense and prosecution; restructured the nature of goings-on in the criminal courtroom; and introduced a more activist conception of what the court system should be trying to accomplish when dealing with the drug-involved offender. By breaking down those barriers and trying to devise a new way of doing things, the Miami innovators opened the door for other jurisdictions to follow suit and to implement versions of treatment drug courts that were in some cases roughly similar to the Miami approach and, in other instances, quite different.

For example, in January 1991, Alameda County, California, established a diversionary treatment drug court in Oakland Municipal Court to intervene with misdemeanor defendants charged with drug violations; they would be diverted to probation for a three-phase program using contingency contracts and frequent in-court reviews of progress. In Multnomah County (Portland), Oregon, during the fall of 1991, the Circuit Court, District Attorney, Public Defender, and staff of a community corrections and a drug treatment program formed a team approach establishing a similar kind of drug court, which targeted defendants entering at the initial stages of criminal processing. Broward County (Fort Lauderdale), Florida, instituted a postadjudication treatment court program in 1991, which focused on first-time felony defendants. Beginning late in 1992, Maricopa County (Phoenix), Arizona, adapted the drug court approach to people convicted of felony possession offenses, borrowed the performance contract approach from the Oakland court, and employed a deferred 60-day jail sentence as a back-up mechanism for encouraging participation in treatment. The Las Vegas Drug Court (in Nevada's Eighth Judicial Circuit) began operation in October, 1992, focusing on drug felonies at the initial stages of processing.

This first generation of treatment drug courts has relied principally on community-based or outpatient forms of drug treatment programming, because they were conceived of as alternatives to traditional processing in the criminal courts and because outpatient modalities were viewed as offering the combination of treatment modalities and other services that were most often appropriate for the types of people entering the drug court programs. In most of these courts, residential treatment, which is much more costly, was employed very selectively. That is not to say that other approaches relying on residential treatment were nonexistent. A related and contemporaneous effort was developed in 1990 by the District Attorney's Office in Kings County (Brooklyn), New York, to divert to residential treatment second-time felony offenders who would otherwise have faced mandatory terms of imprisonment.

Perhaps the most dramatic tribute to the ideas implicit in the original drug court in Miami was the extent of the diffusion of the treatment drug court innovation by the time of the First National Drug Court Conference, held in Miami in December, 1993. At that time, when the pioneering Miami Drug Court was all of 4.5 years old, the drug court "mini" movement already appeared remarkable in both substance and form. One of its striking features was that, although questions about funding and resources were certainly critical to these innovations, virtually none of the principal jurisdictions that had operating drug courts had received federal assistance to implement their programs. Instead, funding approaches for the existing drug courts were generally crafted on the local level, usually in settings where resources for new programs were hard to find. The conference proceedings (Goldkamp, 1994a) revealed that the first-generation efforts had begun to move toward broader and more diverse applications in a second generation, still in the days before federal funding. In Dade County, the innovation kept changing and growing, with an unsuccessful attempt to apply the drug court methodology to sentenced populations to be released from jail for community-based treatment and a very successful attempt to integrate drug treatment court with domestic violence court reforms to address domestic violence offenders who had substance abuse problems (Goldkamp and Weiland, 1996). In New York, the Midtown Community Court was addressing all misdemeanors in a specified geographic area (Times Square) and bringing a wide variety of social services to the courthouse itself. In Kalamazoo, a special court for women offenders brought treatment and other services to bear in a specialized approach. From these roots, in diverse efforts under way in all parts of the United States, central themes and common messages can be identified about a compelling need to draw substance abuse treatment and other community resources into new working relationships with courts to confront the drug problem, its role in crime, and its impact on the community and the criminal justice system. Many of these themes can be traced to—or at least are reflected in—the first treatment drug court in Miami.

Notes

1. The number of arrests for drug violations nationally increased 126% from 1980 to 1989, according to FBI statistics summarized in the *Sourcebooks of Criminal Justice Statistics* published from 1980-1991. See, for example, Naguire, K., and Flanagan, T. (Eds.). (1991). *Sourcebook of Criminal Justice Statistics: 1990.* Washington, DC: U.S. Department of Justice (Table 4.5). There was a slight decline from 1989 to 1990; however, the overall increase from 1980 to 1990 was still 88%. About two thirds of these arrests were for drug possession; one third were for sales or distribution-related offenses [Flanagan, J., and Naguire, K. (1992). *Sourcebook of Criminal Justice Statistics: 1991.* Washington, DC: U.S. Department of Justice].

2. *Diversion* is a term connoting a variety of alternative processing approaches at the preadjudication stage; these have received attention since the 1960s (see the President's Commission on Law Enforcement and Administration of Justice, 1967, pp. 131-134). In 1978, the National Association of Pretrial Services Agencies (1978,

p. 5) defined diversion in its *Performance Standards and Goals for Pretrial Release and Diversion: Diversion* in the following fashion:

1. it offers persons charged with criminal offenses alternatives to traditional criminal justice or juvenile justice proceedings;
2. it permits participation by the accused only on a voluntary basis;
3. the accused has access to counsel prior to a decision to participate;
4. it occurs no sooner than the filing of formal charges and no later than a final adjudication of guilt; and
5. it results in dismissal of charges, or its equivalent, if the divertee successfully completes the diversion process.

3. This account is from the author's notes from participation at a conference entitled, *The Judiciary's Response to the Drug Crisis,* An Executive Symposium of the Court Leadership of the Nine Most Populous States, held April 21 to 22, 1989, in Philadelphia.

4. The reader may wish to consult the complete reporting of findings and description of methodology in other sources. See Goldkamp and Weiland (1993a, 1993b, 1993c).

5. The Miami Drug Court's treatment emphasis has been initially and primarily on outpatient modalities. However, by necessity in 1991, the drug court arranged for prioritized access to more than 200 residential placements for selected defendants with particularly difficult drug abuse problems. As of spring 1993, an average of about 40 such placements were in use at a given moment.

6. The Diversion and Treatment Program is a program of the TASC division of the Office of Rehabilitative Services of Metropolitan Dade County.

7. For a detailed discussion of the design of the research, see Goldkamp and Weiland (1993a, 1993b, 1993c).

8. Elsewhere (Goldkamp and Wieland, 1993b), we have used these data to illustrate how evaluation research can make an important contribution to the further refinement of the treatment drug court innovation in developing differential treatment programming based on classification of entering defendants and in reconsidering target population policy.

9. In fact, the enrollment mechanism was so effective that we discovered that many of the defendants in a planned natural comparison group, defendants ostensibly assigned to drug court but not entering treatment, actually did enter drug court at some point after the sampling period.

10. We should point out that, according to American Bar Association guidelines, diversion is considered a disposition—not an ongoing status. Thus, from a more formal case-processing viewpoint, we could conclude that virtually all of these cases were disposed of within 1 to 3 days, offering a dramatic reduction in time to disposition. The point of our discussion was to show how long the court was typically involved with the cases of drug court defendants.

11. See Gerstein and Harwood, 1990, pp. 11-19, 132-194. We should candidly note that one problem this assessment faces is that there is no obvious or suitable comparison with another comparable program readily available. This problem should be rectified as more jurisdictions implement treatment-oriented drug courts and baseline data are accumulated.

12. For a more in-depth discussion of the definition of favorable outcomes, see the full report (Goldkamp & Weiland, 1993b) and the National Institute of Justice summary (Goldkamp & Weiland, 1993a).

13. For a more in-depth discussion of the definition of favorable outcomes, see the full report (Goldkamp & Weiland, 1993b) and the National Institute of Justice summary (Goldkamp & Weiland, 1993a).

References

American Bar Association. (1993). *The state of criminal justice.* Washington, DC: Author.

Belenko, S. (1990). The impact of drug offenders on the criminal justice system. In R. Weisheit (Ed.), *Drugs, crime, and the criminal justice system* (pp. 27-78). Cincinnati and Hughland Heights: Academy of Criminal Justice Sciences and Anderson Publishing.

Goerdt, J. A., Lomvadias, C., Gallas, G., & Mahoney, B. (1989). *Examining court delay: The pace of litigation in 26 urban trial courts, 1987.* Williamsburg, VA: Bureau of Justice Assistance and the National Center for State Courts, U.S. Department of Justice.

Goerdt, J. A., & Martin, J. A. (1989, Fall). The impact of drug cases on case processing in urban trial courts. *State Court Journal,* pp. 4-12.

Goldkamp, J. S. (1994a). *Justice and treatment innovation: The drug court movement* (A working paper of the First National Drug Court Conference, December 1993). Washington, DC: U.S. Department of Justice, Office of Justice Programs, National Institute of Justice.

Goldkamp, J. S. (1994b). Miami's treatment drug court for felony defendants: Some implications of assessment findings. *The Prison Journal, 73*(2), 110-166.

Goldkamp, J. S., Gottfredson, M. R., & Weiland, D. (1990). Pretrial drug testing and defendant risk. *Journal of Criminal Law and Criminology, 81*(3), 585-652.

Goldkamp, J. S., Jones, P. R., Gottfredson, M. R., & Weiland, D. (1990a). *Assessing the impact of drug-related criminal cases on public safety: Vol. 2. Drug-related recidivism.* Philadelphia: Temple University, Department of Criminal Justice.

Goldkamp, J. S., Jones, P. R., Gottfredson, M. R., & Weiland, D. (1990b). *Assessing the impact of drug-related criminal cases on the judicial process, crowding, and public safety: Vol. 3. Summary and implications.* Philadelphia: Temple University, Department of Criminal Justice.

Goldkamp, J. S., & Weiland, D. (1991). *The impact of court-related practices on the correctional population in Dade County.* Philadelphia: Crime and Justice Research Institute.

Goldkamp, J. S., & Weiland, D. (1993a). *Assessing the impact of Dade County's felony drug court* (Executive summary). Philadelphia: Crime and Justice Research Institute.

Goldkamp, J. S., & Weiland, D. (1993b). *Assessing the impact of Dade County's felony drug court* (Final report). Philadelphia: Crime and Justice Research Institute.

Goldkamp, J. S., & Weiland, D. (1993c). *Assessing the impact of Dade County's felony drug court* (Research in brief). Washington, DC: U.S. Department of Justice, Office of Justice Programs, National Institute of Justice.

Goldkamp, J. S., & Weiland, D. (1996). *The role of drug and alcohol abuse in domestic violence and its treatment: Dade County's Domestic Violence Court experiment.* Final Report to the National Institute of Justice. Philadelphia, PA: Crime and Justice Research Institute.

President's Commission on Law Enforcement and Administration of Justice. (1967). *The challenge of crime in a free society.* Washington, DC: Government Printing Office.

Smith, B. E., Davis, R. C., & Goretsky, S. R. (1991). *Strategies for courts to cope with the caseload pressures of drug cases* (Final report). Washington, DC: American Bar Association.

White House, The. (1989). *National drug control strategy.* Washington, DC: Author.

3. From "Treatment" to "Justice" in Oakland, California

Brooke Bedrick and *Jerome H. Skolnick*

Oakland, California, is home to two drug courts: the Oakland-Piedmont-Emeryville Municipal Court drug court, inaugurated in January 1991 under the leadership of Judge Jeffrey Tauber, and the Alameda County Superior Court drug court,

AUTHORS' NOTE: The authors would like to thank the following individuals for their time and assistance in illuminating the many facets of Oakland's drug courts: Judge Brenda Harbin-Forte; Judge Kenneth R. Kingsbury; Judge Jeffrey S. Tauber; Judge Peggy Hora; Beverly Harris, Director of Adult Services, Alameda County Probation Department; Josefa A. James, Deputy District Attorney, Alameda County; Andrew Hayes, Drug Court Services Coordinator, Oakland Consolidated Drug Courts; Frank Tapia, Probation Officer, Alameda County; Russ Giuntini, Senior Deputy District Attorney in charge of major narcotics prosecution unit, Alameda County; Jim Lee, Senior Deputy District Attorney, Alameda County; Jim Kimzey, Inspector, District Attorney's Office, Alameda County.

inaugurated in January 1995 under the leadership of Judge Martin Jenkins. Both courts target individuals charged with low-level drug felonies, for example, the possession of certain controlled substances (California Health and Safety Code §11350, §11357, and §11358) or the cultivation of marijuana for personal use (California Health and Safety Code Sections §11358). Of these, the Municipal Court drug court (known as Department 3) handles those eligible for drug diversion under California Penal Code §1000, whereas the Superior Court drug court (Department 66) handles those ineligible for diversion under PC §1000 because of a history of similar offenses, a history of the use of violence, or a history of failed drug diversion, among other criteria. Participation in this drug court program requires that the defendant plead guilty to the offense charged and agree to be placed on 3 years of felony probation.

In January 1996, these two drug courts were consolidated. With about 2,000 clients admitted to the consolidated drug courts annually, and with about 2,500 clients on probation through Department 66, these programs—separately as well as together—are among the very largest nationwide (General Accounting Office, 1997, pp. 56-60).[1]

As the size of the program has changed, the rationale of the drug court has shifted subtly but significantly since the Municipal Court program opened its doors on January 2, 1991. Although that program introduced many innovations in handling drug offenses, it responded to the same fiscal constraints and the same frustration with the press of drug cases on the courts that had inspired the organization of an expedited drug court in the 1980s. Although Oakland's drug courts continue to operate with seriously constrained—even inadequate—resources, their programs have become increasingly concerned with the social costs of failed drug policies, especially the loss of generations of African Americans and other people of color to the criminal justice system. One consequence of this reassessment of priorities has been that where the early program sought simply to maximize the length of time it could keep first-time drug offenders from returning to the system and measured success in terms of reduced arrests and time in custody per participant, the program increasingly aspires to increase participants' literacy and educational level, increase job readiness, and even increase the level of employment and income—goals that require an investment of resources.

Race and Justice in Alameda County

Oakland is located in Alameda County—the fourth-densest in population of California's 58 counties (U.S. Bureau of the Census, 1994, pp. 46, 60). Although Caucasians still constitute the majority (> 53%) of the population, African Americans are 17.4% of the population—the highest proportion of African Americans in any California county (AR Associates, 1995, Appendix K-2). Latinos make up 14.5% of the Alameda County population, Asian Americans, 14.2%, and Native Americans, 0.53%. In Oakland—Alameda County's largest city—Caucasians constitute 32.4% of the population, whereas African Americans constitute 43.8%, Asian Americans, 14.7%, and Native Americans, 0.64%. In addition, the census reports that 13.9% of Oakland residents are of Hispanic origin (U.S. Bureau of the Census, 1994, pp. 674-675).

Oakland and Alameda County are remarkable not only for the diversity of their populations but also for the diversity of their municipal and superior court benches, including—perhaps especially—the drug court bench. Five of the forty African American superior court judges statewide sit on the Alameda County Superior Court (where they are 5 of 35 judges, along with one Asian American judge), and 6 of the 48[2] statewide African American municipal court judges sit on the Oakland-Piedmont-Emeryville Municipal Court (where they are 6 of 17 judges, along with one Latino and one Asian American judge). Thus, about 47% of the judges on the Oakland municipal bench are judges of color. The Oakland Municipal Court is also the only municipal court in Alameda County (of six) to have any African American judges (AR Associates, 1995, Appendix B-1 through B-9).[3] Given these statistics, it is remarkable that four of five judges who have presided over Oakland's Municipal Court drug court since its inception and one of two judges presiding over the Superior Court drug court, including the founding judge, are judges of color (three African American women, one African American man, and one Japanese American man)—making Oakland's drug courts perhaps the foremost exception to the perception that justice in California is white.[4] As we shall see, these courts have not been indifferent to the opportunity—and necessity—they face for reconstructing the criminal courtroom as a place where defendants of color feel they will find justice.

Alameda County's War on Drugs

Situated east of the San Francisco Bay and west of the ridge that separates the temperate and frequently foggy Bay Area from the warmer inland regions, and home to the University of California at Berkeley and the polyglot city of Oakland, Alameda County has a deserved reputation for liberal politics. Like many less liberal jurisdictions, however, Alameda County, too, had its 1980s' War on Drugs. This war was effectively inaugurated in the early eighties, when local law enforcement joined forces with federal law enforcement to bring to trial and convict the leaders of Oakland's biggest heroin-dealing gangs—Felix Mitchell and his 69th Avenue Mob, Mickey Moore and his Family, and Harvey Whisenton of Funktown USA. In these prosecutions, the involvement of federal agencies made possible trial in federal court, where speedy trial requirements ensured that the trial would begin within 70 days and where the greatest sentence available was life without possibility of parole—far more punitive than the 4 to 5 years available under state law (Setterberg, 1986, p. 39). This "take no prisoners" approach soon became local policy as well, with the announcement by Alameda County District Attorney John J. Meehan, in July 1984, that thenceforth the policy of his office would be to refuse to plea-bargain felony drug cases and to seek prison terms instead (Greenspan, 1991, pp. 96-97; Setterberg, 1986, p. 40). Indeed, in California from 1985 to 1990, the percentage of drug offenses prosecuted in Superior Court increased steadily from 68.7% to 78.4%, the percentage of these resulting in prison terms increased steadily from 11.4% to 20.3%, and the proportion receiving some jail time hovered around 50% (see Table 3.1).

At the same time, Alameda County, which had relied on federal resources to mount the cases against Mitchell, Moore, and Whisenton (Setterberg, 1986, p. 40), successfully sought state funding for a 2-year pilot project known as the Targeted Urban Crime Narcotics Task Force.[5] In the bill approving funding for this task force, the Legislature found Alameda County

> uniquely situated for this pilot program because of increasing patterns of violent drug gang activities in the urban areas of Oakland and Berkeley. In the last 2 years, 62 drug-related homicides have occurred in Oakland, including two police officers. The courts have been severely impacted

TABLE 3.1 Disposition of Drug Offenses, 1985-1990

Year	*Percentage of Drug Offenses Prosecuted in Superior Court*	*Percentage Sentenced to Prison*	*Percentage Sentenced to Probation With Jail*
1985	68.7	11.4	49.1
1986	72.7	14.8	52.8
1987	74.0	16.2	52.4
1988	76.4	17.5	52.6
1989	78.5	19.5	51.9
1990	78.4	20.3	50.4

SOURCE: California Department of Justice, *Crime and Delinquency in California, 1990.* Tables 39A-39F.

> and there are 450 felony drug cases awaiting preliminary hearing and 250 pending felony drug trials in the Alameda County Superior Court. (Greenspan, 1991, pp. 103-104)

The enumerated provisions of this funding legislation included increasing the enforcement of restrictive conditions of own-recognizance release and bail, increasing the number of trials and convictions in narcotics cases and, especially, decreasing the time between arrest and trial in narcotics cases (Greenspan, 1991, p. 130). According to then-Deputy District Attorney Kenneth Kingsbury, who had been appointed to head the team assembled under the legislation, "Oakland has been a user-friendly community for too long" (Setterberg, 1986, p. 40).

Under Kingsbury, the narcotics task force collaborated with the probation department, the police department, and superior court judges to develop a district attorney-initiated probation revocation process for drug offenders; in effect, it allowed the district attorney's office to seek revocation without charging on the new offense (the arrest for which the police agreed to nullify under California Penal Code Section 849b) while receiving an agreement from the judges to sentence these cases *as if* the defendant had been convicted of the new offense. Prior to this, probation revocation proceedings could be initiated only by the probation department and only subsequent to any hearings on new charges.[6] Kingsbury also developed a broadly worded search clause ensuring that virtually every search of a probationer would be legal. This clause, as read by Kingsbury (personal interview, November 26, 1996) today in the Superior Court drug court, where he now sits on the bench, advises probationers:

> You are to submit to search and seizure by any probation officer, police officer, or any other peace officer at any time of the day or night, with or without a search warrant and with or without probable or reasonable cause, and that will extend to your person, any vehicle under your control, your residence, or any other property under your control.

The combination of this comprehensive search provision, the district attorney-initiated probation revocation process, and the judges' willingness to apply jail or state prison terms to probation revocations increased Alameda County's ability in the 1980s to incarcerate probationers arrested for possession or sale of narcotics. According to data compiled by researcher Rosann Greenspan, the total number of probationers arrested for sales of narcotics increased 123% from 1986 to 1990 (from 102 to 227), whereas the number receiving revocation prison sentences of 3-plus years increased six-fold (12 to 79), although the proportion of sentences these represented fluctuated. The total number of probationers arrested for possession of narcotics tripled from 1986 to 1990 (138 to 390)—in fact, it quadrupled from 1986 to 1989 (to 514), before dropping back by 25% in 1990 (Greenspan, 1991, pp. 172-173).

Establishing a Drug Court in Oakland

It was not only punitive policies that brought increasing numbers of drug cases into Alameda County's criminal justice system. A shift of resources away from the law enforcement-intensive, buy-bust strategy of the mid-1980s narcotics task force era—in which an undercover agent would make the buy and a team observing from a distance would make the bust—and into community policing, for example, resulted in a buy-bust strategy that relied on civilian buyers who were swept up with dealers during the bust (Kingsbury, telephone interview, December 13, 1996). Nor were the 1980s unremittingly punitive. Greenspan's data suggest, for example, that the use of lengthy incarceration sentences for drug-related probation revocation cases rose steadily from 1986 to 1989—and then dropped off steeply and suddenly in 1990.

Although Greenspan doesn't speculate about the source of this sudden shift, the emerging reluctance to impose heavier sentences on repeat petty drug offenders—this retreat from the full-blown punitive policies of the mid-1980s—helped set the stage for the emergence of the drug court,[7] as did other events.

Even at the height of the Alameda County War on Drugs, alternative approaches to the problem of drug-related criminal behavior were in evidence. One such alternative—the Oakland-Piedmont-Emeryville Municipal Court's mentor diversion program—made it possible for men and women 18 to 24 years old accused of felonies, including first-time drug *sellers,* to be diverted and matched with mentors in the community for 18 months to 2 years. Program participants were also required to enroll full-time in community college or adult school, including summer school, and to periodically present the judge with evidence of passing grades. Inaugurated under former Presiding Judge Henry Ramsey to help African American youth avoid becoming convicted felons, successful completion of the program resulted in having the felony charge dropped (Giuntini, telephone interview, December 9, 1996). As of August 1994, 60% of participants were successfully completing the program (Daily Journal Corporation, 1996).

Developing constructive approaches to drug-influenced criminal behavior was also the explicit concern of the Judicial Coordinating Committee (JCC) of Alameda County. In 1986, the JCC, which was charged with advising the Alameda County municipal courts on policy matters, established a subcommittee on driving under the influence (DUI) to investigate the role of alcohol in criminal behavior, state-of-the-art treatment for alcohol and drug dependency, and the efficacy of coerced treatments, among other things (Hora, personal interview, December 10, 1996). By 1989, heroin and cocaine dependencies were so prevalent among defendants coming into the municipal courts that the DUI subcommittee became the Subcommittee on Substance Abuse and DUI.[8] In early 1989, Judge Jeffrey Tauber, who had been elected to the bench in June 1988, joined the JCC substance abuse subcommittee, which he subsequently cochaired with Judge Peggy Hora.[9] The JCC proved a valuable ally in Tauber's efforts to secure the support of other municipal judges for a treatment drug court in Oakland.

In 1990, Judge Tauber had accepted assignment to what was then an expedited drug court. In that court, Tauber took pleas on felony drug cases at a rate of 40 to 50 per week and 10 to 15 minutes per plea, and he oversaw from four to eight preliminary examinations in drug cases per day at 0.5 to 1 hour each. Although California Penal Code §1000 provides for diversion for first-time drug offenders meeting specified conditions, diversion-eligible cases were handled as part of the usual felony arraignment calendar. Drug possession, possession for sale, and diversion failures constituted the bulk of

Tauber's caseload. Indeed, although Tauber found he was putting 10 to 15 people per week back on diversion, his court had no role in ensuring that they received appropriate treatment (Tauber, personal interview, October 26, 1996; telephone conversation, December 15, 1996).

Tauber quickly became frustrated by the senselessness of this system. Expedited drug case-processing techniques had streamlined procedures sufficiently to allow the judge not only to hear more cases in the same amount of time, but also to hear more of the same cases, as offenders cycled rapidly in and out of the expedited drug court. In the fall of 1990, the JCC Subcommittee on Substance Abuse and DUI recommended and the full JCC endorsed a proposal urging the Oakland Municipal Court to undertake a pilot treatment drug court program. Accordingly, Tauber would continue to hear the cases he had heard before, plus all felony diversion cases. The judges of the Oakland-Piedmont-Emeryville Municipal Court accepted the proposal.

With permission to pursue the development of a treatment court, Tauber began to meet jointly with representatives from the District Attorney's office, the Public Defender's office, and the Probation Department. The court was willing to experiment with the handling of drug cases because drug cases were not seen as a priority. With reputation and advancement hinging on how a judge managed complex criminal or civil litigation, routine drug cases were considered a virtual dead-end. For this reason alone, the possibility of allocating all drug cases to the same courtroom was appealing. By contrast, the Probation Department, under the leadership of Robert Norris (at that time head of the adult division), quickly moved from skepticism to active engagement in developing a probation-based treatment program that recognized drug offenders as a priority for the department's limited resources (Tauber, telephone conversation, December 15, 1996). Between the court's amicable indifference and the Probation Department's willingness to innovate, Oakland's Municipal Court drug court was established.

Oakland's Fast, Intensive, Report, Supervision, and Treatment (FIRST) Diversion Program

The diversion program that Tauber inherited fell short for two reasons. First, one third or more of diversion-eligible defendants would fail to return to court for their eligibility hearing—usually scheduled 6 to 8 weeks after their initial court appearance to provide time for a detailed diversion report to be prepared by the Probation Department (Tauber, 1993, p. 6). Second, of those who did return and receive diversion, three fourths would fail to complete the minimal program, largely because of their resistance to meeting with probation officers. In trying to remedy these problems, Tauber faced a third: the lack of resources for designing and implementing a state-of-the-art or tailor-made treatment drug court program. There wasn't—and still isn't—funding in Oakland for the acupuncture treatments that are so popular and apparently effective in a number of other drug courts. Instead, Tauber worked with the Probation Department—"basically, scavenging," as he has put it—to reorganize the drug diversion services into a program that might help participants break their drug dependence and thus their involvement with the criminal justice system.

The defendants targeted for Oakland's FIRST diversion program were almost entirely first-time possession-for-use cases eligible for diversion under California Penal Code §1000. PC §1000 stipulates not only that defendants be first-time drug offenders to be eligible for drug diversion, but also that they have no prior felony conviction within the preceding 5 years, have not been placed on diversion within the preceding 5 years, and have never had parole or probation revoked without subsequently completing it. Most of the defendants Tauber placed in the new diversion program met these criteria, although in some cases, where the defendant had an old drug-related prior, the district attorney agreed to "waive irregularities" and permit entry into the drug diversion program (Tauber, personal interview, October 17, 1996). Of the first 110 defendants to enter the program in 1991, 80% were African American, 78% were male, and 73% were between the ages of 18 and 39—proportions that have generally been representative of the program as a whole (Tauber, 1993, p. D1; Tauber, 1995b).

In a jurisdiction strapped for resources, the court and the Probation Department assembled a treatment drug court program that provided drug-dependent defendants with the following:

1. *Immediate and intensive intervention.* Because the time between first appearance in court and the diversion-eligibility hearing was so great—more than a third of defendants wouldn't make it back to court—and aware of the therapeutic premise that an arrest constitutes a crisis of a few days' duration in the life of an offender during which he or she may respond to interventions normally resisted, Al Chaquette of the Probation Department worked to develop a modi-

fied diversion eligibility report that could be completed overnight, rather than over the 6 to 8 weeks probation officers had spent preparing more extensive diversion reports previously. On the premise that those trying to break their drug dependency need a lot of up-front support, those granted diversion were ordered to report immediately to their probation officer at the Alameda County Probation Department (a 5-minute walk from the municipal court) where they received an orientation to the drug court program and referrals to Narcotics Anonymous (NA) and counseling groups and arranged an NA, counseling, and urinalysis schedule with their probation officer.

Although, per their job description, probation officers had previously weighted their time toward writing reports about rather than actively supervising probationers, they agreed over time to provide a series of five drug education classes and weekly monitoring groups for drug diversion participants.[10] According to Beverly Harris of the Alameda County Probation Department, monitoring groups provide a weekly opportunity for probation officers to check up on participants' progress—whether they are attending counseling, whether they are testing clean—although individual officers may also provide topics for group discussion. The drug education series provides information about the history of drug use in the United States, the effects of drugs on the nervous system, the process of addiction and relapse, and the relationship between drug use and AIDS (Harris, personal interview, November 20, 1996).

2. Contract-based program. Each participant receives a written contract—an innovation developed by Probation Officer Frank Tapia, who had spent a year and a half receiving intensive training in behavioral analysis from two students of B. F. Skinner. This contract outlines the two phases of the diversion program, the specific tasks that must be completed at each phase, the points associated with completing each task, and the incentives that attach to different levels of points. Phase II, for example, as it developed in the treatment drug court, required that over the first 10 weeks of the program, defendants: see their probation officer at least six times (6 points), attend one AIDS education and four drug education classes (5 points), take urine tests (1 point per clean test, maximum of 3 points),[11] register with a community counseling agency (1 point), participate in counseling (1 point per week of participation, maximum of 6 points), and make one payment toward the $220 diversion fee (1 point)—for a total of 22 possible points. The incentives for compliance, which had been painstakingly negotiated between the court, the District Attorney's office, the Public Defender's office, and the Probation Department, were as follows: For a full 22 points, the length of diversion would be reduced from its statutory 24 months to 15 months, and the diversion fee would be reduced from $220 to $120 (a reduction of 9 months and $100); for 18 to 21 points, including two negative urine tests, a reduction of 6 months and $75; for 14 to 17 points, including one negative test and registration for community counseling, a reduction of 3 months and $50. Those with only 11 to 13 points might continue on diversion with the same conditions as long as they were registered for community counseling. Those with 10 points or less might be recycled into diversion Phase II after some time in custody, or they might be terminated, with criminal proceedings reinstated.

This contingency contract, the hallmark of the Oakland drug court program, operates at several levels. By attaching concrete incentives to the requirement to meet regularly with probation, for example, it circumvents the court's initial problem of devising a way to compel participants to meet with probation officers, short of threatening to revoke diversion. By devising in advance the system's response to different levels of participation, it ensures that each player knows in advance and with certainty what the others will do in specific events, allowing them to operate fully as a team. By providing objective criteria for progress through the program, it promotes both a defendant's sense of fairness—each gets the same benefit for the same positive behaviors—and the ability to begin to be responsible for his or her own progress. By specifying incentives but not sanctions, the contract allows the court to respond constructively and with a degree of individuality to the pitfalls of drug dependency.

3. A "reality-based" program. If the contingency contract is the hallmark of the Oakland drug court, the notion that an effective drug court program is "reality-based" is its foundational principle. Early on, Tauber summarized the rationale for a reality-based drug rehabilitation program as follows:

> Successful court-ordered drug rehabilitation programs are based on an understanding of the physiological, psychological, and behavioral realities of drug usage and are designed and implemented with those realities in mind. They recognize that drug usage is a serious debilitating disease; that relapse and intermittent progress are a part of most successful drug rehabilitation; that as a drug addiction is not created overnight, it cannot be cured overnight; that a drug user is most vulnerable to successful intervention when he or she is in crisis (i.e., immediately after initial

> arrest and incarceration); that drug users are in denial and will do everything possible to avoid responsibility, make excuses for program failure, and evade the court and its programs. The FIRST Diversion Program is an attempt to work with, rather than against, those realities (Tauber, 1993, p. 3).

In practice, this acknowledgment of the realities of drug dependency has meant that program participants could continue to use drugs, or return to using, without necessarily being terminated from the program. Instead, a range of sanctions are employed, from having a defendant spend the morning or the day in the jury box, watching and possibly learning some lessons from what transpires, to increasing the weekly counseling or NA meetings required, decreasing the time to the next court appearance, or placing the defendant in custody for one or a few days—just to think things over.

It would be a mistake, however, to understand this range of sanctions as a lenient alternative to taking a defendant's drug use seriously. Instead, the availability of a range of sanctions makes it possible for the court to impose sanctions progressively, communicating to the defendant and, indeed, to the entire courtroom of defendants and other observers that, as Tauber (personal interview, October 27, 1996) puts it, "not only are we serious but they should be serious as well."

> An offender comes in to talk to me in court and says, "I'm ready, I've just had a revelation here in court." My feeling is—they're scared, they want to avoid jail. They may have some notion that their life hasn't been good, but I don't think that they have any commitment to a sober lifestyle. I think that develops over time, and very often it takes some significant sanctions to convince them.

Tauber is especially frustrated by judges who repeatedly threaten defendants for continued drug use without invoking any sanctions, and then suddenly snap and send them to state prison. In this situation, Tauber (personal interview, October 27, 1996) says,

> There's no warning, there's no system, there's no reason for this person to believe that they're going to state prison for a failure, because the judge hasn't taken it seriously to that point. And of course the judge thinks that he has or she has been very reasonable and considerate and bent over backwards—and has given all the wrong messages.

Although no data exist on how sanctions were employed in Tauber's courtroom, observation of Oakland's Municipal Court drug court today suggests that from one quarter to one third of those appearing before the judge on any given day may receive some sort of sanction—from a warning that each dirty drug test over the next progress report period will result in 1 day in custody, to requiring that the participant enter a residential program as a condition of continuing in the program, to requiring submission to a urine test during the court's recess, to remanding the defendant to the custody of the court for that day or to the custody of the sheriff overnight or longer. Here's how Tauber (personal interview, October 27, 1996) has described the drug court's rule of thumb on sanctions: "It never seemed appropriate to me to sanction people for drug use. It seemed very appropriate to sanction people for failure to comply with an order."

In the reality-based courtroom, reality means both that the court recognizes the difficulties of the defendant's situation and that the defendant understands the consequences of failure to fulfill contractual obligations. The following demonstrates how stark this reality can be: On the Wednesday before Thanksgiving of 1996, Judge Brenda Harbin-Forte of Oakland's Municipal Court drug court, remanded into the custody of the sheriff a man who had sole custody of his two young children, because his drug tests had continued to come up dirty. Judge Harbin-Forte clearly hesitated before imposing the order, asking a number of questions of the man and the probation officer, while struggling to decide how to proceed. But, as she reminded the defendant and the others in the court, she had agreed at his last court appearance that he could continue on diversion in spite of his dirty urine tests on the condition that if these continued, he would spend the Thanksgiving holiday in custody. "You've been using throughout and we cut that deal at your request," she told the defendant. "Guess I'm not going to cut any more deals in this case." When the public defender, observing that the court "shouldn't punish the kids," announced that he had just gotten the defendant's baby-sitter on the phone and she, too, would not be available to take care of the kids over the holiday, the judge responded, demonstrating how serious this developing situation was: "There's always child protective services, which seems to be what he has in mind for his children anyway." "I wish you would get your act together," she told the defendant. "You just cannot be a proper parent with drugs around" (Court Session, November 27, 1996).

In the treatment courtroom, this reality check is offered not only for the benefit of the defendant, but for the benefit as well of all those in the courtroom on that day. Tauber (1993, p. 6), for example, carefully arranged his court calendar "to provide an object lesson to participants on the potential consequences of the program," with failures appearing first, those making progress reports second, admissions to diversion third, and finally, after new admissions had left the courtroom, those being recycled or reinstated into the program. Similarly, in Harbin-Forte's courtroom, graduations occur twice a week at the top of the program, followed by progress reports and admissions to diversion, including a motivational address by the judge. In-custody cases are heard after the morning recess, when all those appearing for progress reports or admission have left except those remanded to the custody of the court for that day.

4. *An ability to make a virtue of necessity.* With limited human and financial resources available for developing the treatment drug court, not every feature of Oakland's program fulfills a therapeutic purpose. Some features are dictated, quite simply, by necessity. Those implementing the treatment drug court, however, appear always ready to envision therapeutic rationales for pragmatic practices. Thus, for example, an innovation designed by Al Chaquette of the Probation Department to allow probation officers to manage their time more efficiently—namely, placing the four probation officers assigned to supervise drug divertees on weekly rather than daily rotations in the courtroom—was soon recognized as a "brilliant" addition to the FIRST program:

> All of a sudden, the probation officer is in court when the person is put on probation. So they have seen the probation officer in court. Then they see him or her at orientation. And every 5 weeks, the probation officer is back in court, so if someone screws up, the case can be followed up at week five, instead of waiting 10 weeks. (Tauber, personal conversation, October 27, 1996)

According to Tauber, the development of this sort of reliable relationship is widely thought to encourage a sense of mutual accountability that is therapeutically beneficial—although further cuts in Probation Department resources have since brought an end to this particular innovation. Similarly, the decision to have probation officers meet with drug divertees in groups rather than individually—an innovation introduced by Probation Officer Frank Tapia—was intended simply to reduce workloads but was soon perceived as adding a much-needed group-counseling element to the program. Group counseling reportedly circumvents challenges to the probation officer's credibility on issues relating to drugs he or she has not used because others in the group can speak from personal experience and, as Beverly Harris (personal interview, November 20, 1996) has put it, "cut right through the games" fellow drug addicts may play.

In short, the early Oakland drug court was not in the business of implementing a series of therapeutic principles and practices designed in advance of its operation, but rather in the business of forging a program within the limits of what was financially and practically feasible at any given time. The anticipation that elements of the program will change as new strategies are devised to maximize the effects of limited financial and human resources is consequently built into the program. Indeed, this feature of the program is itself always cast positively—as a productive responsiveness to local circumstances—which to some extent it is. There is also, however, a widespread tacit understanding that making a virtue of necessity is, at base, just an optimistic form of making do with resources inadequate to the real tasks at hand.

Assessing Oakland's Initial Drug Court Program: The Numbers

These, then, are the elements of the drug court program as it was established in 1991: a probation department diversion team reorganized to provide immediate diversion-eligibility assessments, group programs, and weekly contacts over the course of the program; a contingency contract, providing concrete incentives for compliance with the requirements of the program; a principled commitment by the court team to respond constructively to the realities of drug dependency; and a general willingness to envision therapeutic rationales for pragmatic arrangements, so that no elements would be purely practical.

The little data available suggest that these innovations in Oakland's drug diversion program did make some difference. The principal source of data is an in-house comparison of the first 110 defendants entering the old, nondrug court diversion program in 1990 with the first 110 entering the new treatment drug court diversion program (the FIRST program) in 1991.[12] The fate of these 220 individuals was assessed at 24 months, 36 months, and 48 months from arraignment, with data collected on new felony arrests since arraignment and total number of days in custody on felony offenses during each year of the study. The 1990 sample was 80% male, 87% African American, 6% Caucasian, and 6% Other. The 1991 sample was 78% male, 80% African American, 12% Caucasian, and 8% Other (Tauber, 1995a).

The data show that of those entering the program in 1991, 97% appeared in court for their diversion eligibility hearing, compared with only 64% of the 1990 group, suggesting that the quick turnaround between first court appearance and the eligibility hearing inaugurated by the FIRST program was effective. In an explicit effort by the court not to skim the most promising cases for the program, Tauber (1993, pp. 11-12, 15) admitted a much higher proportion of those meeting minimal eligibility criteria than had been admitted to drug diversion in the previous year (86.6% compared with 65.9%), extending the benefit of the doubt where the earlier program would have played it safe. Nonetheless, nearly twice as many of the 1991 sample successfully completed the program—54% compared with only 29% of the 1990 sample.

Looking at the rearrest, 55% of those entering drug diversion in 1990 had a new felony arrest within 36 months of arraignment, compared with 41% of those entering the FIRST program in 1991—a statistically significant difference at the .05 level (Tauber, 1995a). By the fourth year, however, the gap between the two samples was closing, with 55% of the 1990 sample and 47% of the 1991 sample showing new felony arrests within 48 months of arraignment (see Table 3.4). The fourth year data also show 41% of the women in the 1990 sample (n = 22) and 42% of the women in the 1991 sample (n = 24) were rearrested at 48 months (Tauber, 1995b).

This reduction in the difference between outcomes for the two groups over time is also evident in the data on total days in custody on felony offenses, as are further anomalous results for female program participants. For male participants in the FIRST program, total days in custody on felony offenses was 54% lower in Year 1 than for their 1990 counterparts, although the difference between the groups decreased over time (see Table 3.2). By contrast, all female participants in the FIRST program spent 13.2% *more* days in custody during Year 1 than did female drug divertees in 1990 (see Table 3.3) whereas African American women (n = 19) in the FIRST program spent 60.6% more days in custody than their 1990 counterparts (see Table 3.4). Female participants also fared worse on diversion in general: Of the 1990 sample, 31% of the men but only

TABLE 3.2 Time in Custody for Men, Before and After the FIRST Program

Interval Since Arraignment	*Total Days in Custody* 1990 Offenders (N = 88)	1991 Offenders (N = 86)	*Percentage Change*
Year 1	3,160	1,440	–54
Year 2	2,734	1,450	–47
Year 3	1,532	1,005	–34.4
Year 4	981	767	–21.8

SOURCE: Data provided by Judge Jeffrey S. Tauber. 1990 offenders were handled under the old diversion program; 1991 offenders were handled under the new treatment drug court program, FIRST.

TABLE 3.3 Time in Custody for Women, Before and After the FIRST Program

Interval Since Arraignment	*Total Days in Custody* 1990 Offenders (N = 22)	1991 Offenders (N = 24)	*Percentage Change*
Year 1	317	359	+13.2+
Year 2	533	309	–42
Year 3	273	260	–4.8
Year 4	445	74	-83%

SOURCE: Data provided by Judge Jeffrey S. Tauber. 1990 offenders were handled under the old diversion program; 1991 offenders were handled under the new treatment drug court program, FIRST.

TABLE 3.4 New Felony Arrests, Before and After the FIRST Program

Interval Since Arraignment	*Percentage of Defendants With Felony Arrests* 1990 Offenders (N = 110)	1991 Offenders (N = 110)	*Percentage Change*
Year 1	35	18	–49
Year 2	—	—	—
Year 3	55	41	–25
Year 4	55	47	–15

SOURCE: Data provided by Frank Tapia. 1990 offenders were handled under the old diversion program; 1991 offenders were handled under the new treatment drug court program, FIRST.

23% of the women successfully completed the program; of the 1991 sample, 57% of the men but only 42% of the women successfully completed.

Further evidence of generally positive outcomes for FIRST program participants comes from the National Center for State Courts (NCSC, 1996), which recently undertook a brief analysis of outcomes for a larger, more statistically valid sample of 500 FIRST participants entering the program between 1991 and 1994. The NCSC found that from the time they entered the program in 1991 until March 1996, fully 60% of the 1991 sample had no felony arrests, 87.4% had no felony convictions, and another 10.2% had only one felony conviction. Of the sample entering the program in 1992, 83.2% had no felony arrests by March 1996, and 94.8% had one or no felony convictions. While these numbers are impressive, without comparison data for pre-FIRST diversion program drug divertees, it is, of course, impossible to assess how much to attribute these results to the program.

Assessing Oakland's Initial Drug Court Program: Innovations, Continuities

With the introduction of the FIRST diversion program in January 1991, more people showed up for their diversion eligibility hearing, more were placed on diversion, and more completed diversion successfully. New felony arrests and days in custody on felony offenses dropped significantly on the whole, although the improvements demonstrated by the 1991 sample in comparison with the 1990 sample decreased substantially over time—an outcome, it should be noted, which may well be attributable to the lack of any significant aftercare services.[13] In general, women appeared to fare considerably worse than men, although the sample is too small to support reliable inferences about outcomes by sex for the population as a whole. The majority of program participants had no new felony arrests a full 4 years after entering the program, and more than 80% had no new felony convictions.

In addition to the specific program elements described above, the innovations implemented in achieving these results included a fundamental alteration in the relationship between the judge and the defendant, which appears characteristic of treatment courts generally. In the expedited drug court setting, in Oakland as elsewhere, this relationship had been intrinsically a matter of indifference. Concern with rendering the processing of drug cases more efficient had focused the court's attention on the similarities between cases rather than their differences. In the treatment court, by contrast, a growing concern with rendering the outcome of drug cases more effective—that is, with rehabilitating defendants so they do not reoffend—has required that the court increasingly take cognizance of the defendant as an individual. What had been an impersonal drug court process has thus become a personalized interaction concerning individual outcomes. Tauber (personal interview, October 26, 1996) has summed up the difference between the FIRST program and what preceded it: "Creating a system which the offender could succeed in had been low priority. Now it became top."

The shift of attention from case processing to case outcome occasioned another so-called innovation, also widely considered characteristic of treatment courts in general: the reconceptualization of previously adversarial or competitive court players as members of a court team working together to help the defendant rehabilitate. In Oakland, at the outset, this team consisted of the public defender, the district attorney, the bench, and the probation department, as the designated treatment provider. According to Tauber (personal interview, October 27, 1996), the process of "redefining how we work together" was perhaps the single most important transformation initiated by the treatment court. As he explains,

> Well, yes, there's immediacy, there's sanctions, there's incentives. But I think very often it's that you've got a team that's working together, that has some pride in its effectiveness and ability to make things happen [that makes the difference]. That for the first time, probation officers are actually sitting down with the judge before cases and going over cases where there is interplay and discussion and argument.

In retrospect, however, the early drug court's continuities with what had preceded it are perhaps just as apparent as its innovations. For example, although the expedited drug court operated impersonally whereas the treatment court operates personally, both courts are oriented toward removing drug cases from the criminal justice system as efficiently and, especially, as economically as possible. This attention to economy is apparent in the criteria Tauber's court applied in assessing its own early success—the proportion of completions and the reductions in days in custody and new felony arrests—as well as in Tauber's translation of these reductions into cost-savings for the criminal justice system in his second-year report. In particular, Tauber (1993, p. 22) claimed substantial system-wide savings ($2 million-plus) based on unused jail beds, which the Alameda County Sheriff's Department rented to the San Francisco

Sheriff's Department and to the U.S. Immigration and Naturalization Service.

Although the FIRST diversion program undoubtedly contributed to the availability of jail beds in Alameda County, the notion that money spent incarcerating petty drug offenders was money wasted both preceded and, in a sense, transcended the FIRST program, as did policies designed to reduce the presence of low-level drug offenders in Alameda County jails. We have already seen, for example, that the length of probation revocation jail sentences dropped sharply between 1989 and 1990 and that a successful alternative to incarceration for first-time drug sellers, among others, was already operating at the time the FIRST diversion program was established. As an economical measure, the FIRST program was thus of a piece with other efforts to stanch the flow of limited resources into an exponentially expanding criminal justice system.

As drug policy, too, the FIRST program signaled more of a shift in means—from modifying drug-using behavior through punishment to modifying it through coerced treatment—than a reconceptualization of ends. The notion—widely used as a justification for Oakland's treatment court and for other treatment courts as well—that "just locking up people for drug use isn't working, so we might as well try something else" argues for alternatives to incarceration, certainly, but leaves unexamined the premise that the program's goal is simply a nonoffending population—rather than, say, a job-ready or literate or employed population. Indeed, as we have seen, the goals of the early FIRST diversion program were simple: Finish the program, no new arrests, and as few days in custody as possible. This focus on modifying behavior rather than on positively addressing the factors undergirding drug use is also apparent in the FIRST program's annual reports.[14]

Finally, as treatment, the early FIRST diversion program was essentially a patchwork of services available in the community, supplemented by the few weekly group sessions put on by the Probation Department, not something created anew. Indeed, according to Beverly Harris (personal interview, November 20, 1996) of the Alameda County Probation Department, the department's drug education classes "basically are didactic. They're not in any way counseling per se, although there may be some minimal interaction," while the monitoring groups, too, are less therapeutic than simply practical opportunities for "touching base." As Harris puts it, "as probation officers we are not therapists." Meanwhile, general counseling and NA counseling services depended not only on what was available in the community, but—even more restricted—on what members of the drug court team knew about available community services. At that time, there was no drug court coordinator charged with developing community service resources. The amalgamated quality of the treatment component of the program had its own therapeutic justification (again, virtue of necessity) in the notion propounded, says Tauber (personal interview, October 27, 1996), by "a lot of people who are significant players . . . that the most important thing is to maintain contact with the offender on a frequent basis; it almost doesn't matter what the content of the treatment is." Even today, Tauber reports, "I'm not sure exactly what treatment is. What cures one person is not going to cure another. There's a lot we still don't know."

In short, a retrospective assessment of Oakland's initial treatment drug court suggests that its genius lay not in the degree to which it broke with the past, but rather in the degree to which it was able to reconfigure elements of extant theories, practices, and personnel into a drug diversion program that maximized the effects of these limited financial and human resources. Having said this, it is important to say as well that several elements of this reconfigured program—its contractual language, its commitment to acknowledging realities, and its supportive drug court team—have subsequently taken on lives of their own, as it were, giving shape to a drug court program that is today perhaps as removed from the initial treatment court program as that program was from what preceded it.

Oakland's Drug Courts Today

The Superior Court Drug Court Program

The single most obvious difference between Oakland's initial drug court program and the program today is that a treatment court now operates at the Superior Court level as well as at the Municipal Court level. As described at the outset, the Superior Court program (Department 66) provides 3 years of probation for drug possession-for-use cases ineligible for diversion under PC §1000. While the Department 66 program shares some elements with the Municipal Court program, it also differs from it in some respects.

Like the Municipal Court, Department 66 relies on the Probation Department to supervise program participants and connect them with community-based services. A different group of probation officers works with these drug probationers than works with the drug divertees, but probationers receive the same drug and AIDS education series and the same monitoring groups that divertees do. The Probation Department also runs some process groups specifically for Department 66 clients, where probation officers "actually help [clients] work through some of the issues that bring them into the criminal justice system" (Harris, personal interview, November 20, 1996). Like the Municipal Court, Department 66 provides incentives for compliance with program conditions. Unlike the Municipal Court program, these incentives are not attached to point-based behaviors specified in a written contract, but rather are verbally specified by the judge (Kingsbury, personal interview, November 26, 1996). Department 66 also differs in that its participants, who have all pled guilty to felony drug offenses, remain in custody several weeks before entering the program, while a full presentencing report is developed. They are also subject, as drug divertees are not, to the comprehensive search clause mentioned above.

The same things that make Department 66 participants ineligible for diversion—substantial criminal histories, long-standing drug dependency, previous failures at diversion or probation—also make them a more difficult population to treat. According to Beverly Harris (personal interview, November 20, 1996),

> The diversion cases tend to have more of their life together still than the convicted felons. . . . Diversion people have not had as much exposure to treatment as people who have been convicted may have. The people who have been convicted may already have gone through the whole diversion thing and still not have dealt with their substance abuse. Because people on diversion are still working or have a source of income, they may not be involved in peripheral kinds of criminal activity. They may be more hopeful than folks who have been convicted. They have more to look forward to.

A single episode, from Judge Kingsbury's courtroom, dramatizes the scope of the problem some of these offenders pose. Somber during the morning recess because he had had to remand to custody a woman who had unilaterally moved out of her residential treatment program, in order to underscore to other program participants—a largely capricious lot—that they must abide by the conditions laid down by the court, Kingsbury explained that the decision had been difficult because he had known this particular woman over the course of more than 25 years—from the time he was a young probation officer, through his years in the district attorney's office, and now as a judge. "In fact," he said, "I'll never forget the first night I met her, now so many years ago: the night she killed her father." Since that time, she had not committed a single act of violence, although her drug dependency had persisted, and perhaps deepened (Court Session, October 17, 1998).

Offenders with personal histories this long and this troubled are rare among Department 66 participants, but even those with half this history present a stiff challenge to a treatment drug court. Indeed, such a population was not even contemplated at the outset of the FIRST diversion program, which was premised, as we have seen, on the theory that "out of th[e] crisis [engendered by a first in-custody experience] comes our best (and perhaps last) opportunity for successful intervention" (Tauber, 1993, p. 2). Without any data available, it is impossible to assess just how stiff this challenge is. It is clearly apparent from what goes on in the courtroom, however—the many failures to appear (which result in probation being revoked and a bench warrant issued), the struggling probationers who ask the judge to let them serve their time in custody in lieu of probation, the severely disoriented young man who literally stumbled into the courtroom an hour after his case was called and demanded to know why he was there—that many offenders find the program a steep uphill battle.

The myriad, idiosyncratic ways in which these probationers struggle is one reason a concrete contract has not been employed in Department 66. The need to ensure that trying and failing does not result in more severe consequences than not trying at all has been another impediment to developing a written, point-based contract for this population. As Beverly Harris (personal interview, November 20, 1996) observes:

> In diversion, what's going to happen to you if you fail is that your diversion is terminated and criminal proceedings are reinstated. A whole lot of things can happen when criminal proceedings are reinstated. But in Superior Court drug court—you're a convicted felon. What happens to you when you fail is that you go to prison. And that's a tremendous consequence for a dirty test!. . . We don't want this population to have to suffer severe consequences that other folks who are not in the drug court would not suffer. It's a real challenge.

Nonetheless, some sort of point-based contract specifying incentives and sanctions is currently in the process of having it's *i*'s dotted and *t*'s crossed. Two additional changes will accompany the implementation of a written contract in Department 66. First, the drug court team will undertake measures to better distinguish "actual crooks for whom substance use is incidental, from folks with actual substance abuse problems for whom criminal behavior is incidental" (Kingsbury, telephone interview, December 13, 1996). One such measure may be to wait until the first progress report to grant entry into the program. By more carefully guarding entry to the program, the court expects to reduce the number of program participants significantly, from about 950 to about 350 (Kingsbury, telephone conversation, December 13, 1996). Those offenders not admitted to the program will be placed on probation for the full 3 years—where they are subject to probation search conditions and probation revocation proceedings, as described above—but they will be supervised only minimally. A middle group, with histories suggesting they pose some risk, will receive closer supervision, but not the intensive support provided those in the drug court program.

The second change the court plans to implement is to invest more heavily in the participants that it does admit—"giving some folks a quarter, rather than trying to give everybody a dime," as Kingsbury (telephone conversation, December 13, 1996) puts it. If Kingsbury has his preferences—that is, if the court manages to secure the grants or other funding it needs to begin to actually invest in assisting drug probationers—he would like to see resources put into pre-release planning, job readiness, and actual job placement. Plans are also under way to initiate some sort of graduation ceremony for those completing the program (unlike the Municipal Court drug court, none is currently in place) and to include program graduates in joint drug court-police department presentations to local high schools.

The Municipal Court Drug Court Program

Oakland's Municipal Court drug court has changed substantively since it started in 1991, although some broad continuities with the earlier program are apparent. The contingency contract, for example, is very close to the one developed during Tauber's tenure. The points required for completing each phase have been increased (to 33); the number of urinalysis tests required during Phase II have increased (from three to six); Phase II has itself been extended from 10 to 12 weeks; and placement in a residential treatment program has been added as an alternative to short-term custody or termination for failing to accumulate sufficient points during the first attempt at Phase II. The contract itself, however, remains a cornerstone of the program. The Probation Department continues to provide the same drug education classes and monitoring groups as previously. Recent legislation requires a guilty plea and deferred entry of judgment as a condition of eligibility for drug diversion, unless an agreement is reached between the court, the District Attorney, and the Public Defender that a drug court will be run as a pre-guilty plea diversion program. The Oakland Municipal Court drug court team has reached this agreement. Accordingly, the program will, for the most part, continue operating as it has, although some participants will be required to submit guilty pleas.[15]

Now, however, addressing defendants' substance abuse is only the beginning, not the end of the court's purpose:

> We've come a long way as far as the substance abuse part goes. But all those other parts are still not being touched: the educational piece that makes people employable, gives them skills; the employment piece; the family systems piece. All those pieces are yet to be really addressed.
>
> What we have addressed effectively is the substance abuse: . . . how to deal with it. But as people become sober and maintain their sobriety, there are all those other pieces. When we look at the community-based organizations that are involved in the drug court at this moment, they are organizations that deal with substance abuse, not organizations that deal with employability or family systems. I think that's coming—but that's where we need to go. (Harris, personal interview, November 20, 1996)

Accordingly, the realities that the sympathetic, nonadversarial drug court team takes cognizance of now encompass the participant's social relations and responsibilities as well as his or her individual physiological and psychological states. These realities include the difficulties of meeting the multiple weekly requirements of drug diversion when one is a low-level employee in one, or two, or three jobs; the difficulty of keeping a job when one is in an unstable, or violent, living situation; as well as the difficulty of abstaining from drugs through any number of the various tragedies and dislocations that so often afflict the poor and very poor.

The Oakland drug court's goal or vision, in other words, has become not simply to remove people from the criminal justice system, but, more positively, to help them find a productive place in the community. Toward this end, Judge Brenda Harbin-Forte, who sat on Oakland's Municipal Court drug court bench for 1995 and 1996, regularly required that drug divertees participate in literacy, GED-preparation, or college classes, as appropriate—an innovation she undertook because the absence of systematic attention to education and employment troubled her. "People only rise to the level of expectations," she explains:

> Many people from the inner cities have been given the message that they are expected to end up as criminals. They have low self-esteem and no positive role models or reinforcement. But in fact, virtually every person coming through this court is capable of rising considerably higher than they usually do. (Harbin-Forte, personal interview, October 18, 1996)

In 1995, the court began to build connections with community-based organizations focused on employment and employability. One important result has been the hiring of a drug court services coordinator, who is responsible for locating and developing employment opportunities for drug court participants. Meanwhile, to foster civic involvement, the court is in the process of initiating a volunteer work requirement in lieu of the diversion fine which, according to Beverly Harris, would ideally be met by having program participants approaching graduation serve as mentors for people entering the program.

These new goals require new criteria for success. Beverly Harris (personal interview, November 20, 1996), for example, suggests that employment level, income level, educational level, and degree of civic involvement, at the beginning of a divertee's program and at its end, might provide a more appropriate measure of success than urine tests and recidivism. "Sure you don't want people committing additional crimes," she comments. "Definitely. But look at other things as well." These new goals also require resources—not maximizing minimal resources or making a virtue of necessity, which characterized the early drug court program—but, as is increasingly the case in the Superior Court program as well, an actual investment of resources.

One step toward this end has been for the court to begin pursuing federal funding. Another step has been to inaugurate a drug court steering committee composed of representatives from relevant county agencies, community-based organizations, and the court to facilitate court-community collaboration in the development and distribution of services. A third has been to begin thinking about having the Probation Department itself provide direct services to drug court participants. "Sometimes," Harris (personal interview, November 20, 1996) explains,

> Community agencies, because of their limited resources, pick and choose who will benefit from their resources. And our population is not always at the top of the list. So to that extent, we need to offer some services as well. . . . And to tell you the truth, since everybody is pinched so much, everyone has said "whatever you can do to help is great."

The move toward investing significant resources in drug court program participants changes the relationship between the court and the community. Where, traditionally, community organizations have concerned themselves with the law-abiding while the court has addressed itself to the law-violating, Oakland's emerging drug court program anticipates an arrangement in which the court and the community share responsibility for those on the right and the wrong sides of the law. Harris (personal interview, November 20, 1996) acknowledges, for example, that she can imagine the Probation Department one day providing services to community members regardless of whether they have violated any laws, much as the Community Court and Justice Center currently under development in the Red Hook section of Brooklyn, New York, anticipates providing some services to the community at-large (Midtown Community Court, n.d.). She is also interested in "collaborating with other people who know about employability[,] . . . collaborating with private industry," to provide the probation population with services they need but are not getting. "There is no space any more for 'them and us' in the field of human services," Harris explains, "for turf wars. . . . Because you can't afford to have people not get the services that they need. When they don't get them, everybody suffers." Judge Peggy Hora (personal interview, December 10, 1996), an ardent proponent of treatment drug courts, echoes these sentiments. "Turf wars are a thing of the past," she explains. "Today, the time for cooperation is ripe like no other."

The move to investing resources in the drug court programs also entails a redefinition of the relationship between the court and the defendant, which, by extension, redefines the relationship between those on the margins of the law and those at its center. Where the relationship between the judge and the defendant in the early drug court program was literally contractual, this relationship has become—in the Superior Court from the beginning and increasingly in the Municipal Court—symbolic as well.[16] The FIRST diversion program's written contract was originally developed—and appears to have worked effectively—as a behavior modification tool. The use of contractual language in today's drug court programs communicates how one engages in a contractual relationship and the mutual obligations and benefits that attach not only to discrete, point-based behaviors, but also to the relationship between the court and defendant. Thus, a judge may keep up his or her end of a verbal deal in spite of reservations, may reduce sanctions in exchange for honesty, and will frequently urge program participants to be businesslike in their interactions with the court. Moreover, the court represents this relationship as inhering in shared experience. In an address she offers to entering program participants, for example, Judge Harbin-Forte encourages them to recognize similarities between her life and theirs and, by extension, to see themselves as potentially productive members of the community: "You look up here and see me wearing this black robe—having a pretty good life, you think," she begins,

> You may think I don't know what it is like to struggle. But I've had to overcome obstacles to be sitting here as a judge. Poverty. Injustice. Discrimination. Teen pregnancy. I had a son when I was just 16 years old and living in Mississippi, where I wasn't supposed to make anything of myself.
>
> I could have used these things as excuses, but I didn't. I decided I would still try to do something with my life. So when I don't buy your excuses, it's not because I don't care—I do—but because I know you can do better. I know what it is to carry burdens. But I also know how good it feels to accomplish goals. (Court Session, October 23, 1996)

At graduation she tells participants, "I hope to never see you in the criminal justice system again—but do come back and visit and let us know how you're doing. The Court is still here for you, the Probation Department is still here for you." (Indeed, on a few occasions program graduates did stop by the courtroom to say hello, including one young woman with a healthy, drug-free newborn). The relationship between the court team and the program participants, in other words, transcends the courtroom although it may begin there. According to a reliable insider, even the experience of being in recovery may be something that some drug court team members share with court clients.

Although all court players acknowledge that some offenders are "truly criminals" who, in Harris's words, "deserve to be locked up forever and a day," the operating assumption is that most program participants are like other members of society. "For the most part," says Harris (personal interivew, November 20, 1996), "these are folks that we are interacting with every day, and we just don't know it." As she puts it, recounting her response to Pacific Gas and Electric when they refused to lease space to the Probation Department because they didn't want "that population" coming in: "Our population are your clients. Those are people you serve. . . . So, how do you know this is not 'your' population? We need to get people to understand that the distinctions are really not as severe as they've been told."

Nor, as alluded to at the outset, are the drug court team and its program participants bifurcated on the basis of race. Although the great majority of program participants are people of color, the majority of judges who have sat on the drug court bench are as well, as are other members of the drug court team. Although the view that offenders of color respond better to authorities of color remains somewhat controversial, as Deputy District Attorney Josefa James (personal interview, December 11, 1996), herself of mixed race, states simply: "It just wouldn't work in this day and age for white folks to be deciding the future for people of color."

What does divide drug court offenders from the drug court team and by extension the law-abiding segment of society is largely access to the institutional resources necessary for abiding by the law.[17] As stated by the Commission on the Future of the California Courts (1993), in a report frequently alluded to by drug court team players,

> Although crime may not have social causes, it clearly has social correlates. . . . . [I]t is the children who grow up in poverty today who will commit much of the crime tomorrow.
>
> . . . . [I]f California is . . . to have a future in which there is *less* crime—not merely better-controlled crime—then society and the government must redouble their efforts to address effectively those social problems that are crime's correlates. (pp. 150-151)

Indeed, in this context, incarcerating low-level offenders appears a costly misallocation of severely limited resources. Among the "negative scenarios" suggested to the commission, as it held hearings up and down the state on the future of the courts, were "those in which social disintegration has been so complete that the courts no longer have authority or purpose and have been either co-opted or suppressed by the powerful" or

> not quite so apocalyptic, . . . a future in which there are essentially no resources at all for the courts (or any other branch of government), in which the only justice is private, governing relations among the rich while the underclass exists in virtual anarchy. (pp. 7-8)

Currently, the court's ability to connect participants to job training and to actual jobs is inadequate—despite the remarkable resourcefulness of Judge Jenkins, for example, as he went door-to-door, at times successfully, seeking work for his probationers. Nevertheless, it appears to be increasingly taken as given that the court has a role to play in developing access to employment, education, and other institutionally provided resources on the grounds that it is, simply, unjust to apply punishment to low-level drug offenders who have not yet had the benefit of access to such resources. The court is emphatic that neither a lack of access to resources nor the impediments that race or ethnicity may entail will be tolerated as excuses. To an African American defendant pleading the difficulties of a black man in America, Deputy District Attorney James retorted, "Certainly you are not asking me to believe that because you are a black man you have no responsibility to stay off drugs, no responsibility to care for your children, no responsibility to keep them out of the system or to set a good example for them—are you?" Or, as Judge Harbin-Forte puts it, "Even those for whom life is a considerable struggle have a responsibility to rise as high as they can." If justice requires that the court provide defendants access to the resources and opportunities they need to make positive changes in their lives, it also requires that defendants assume the responsibilities these opportunities entail. The court will consider criminal and subject to punishment those who, once provided this access, shirk responsibility or opt to break the law. As Harbin-Forte tells entering drug divertees, "Nobody goes to jail in this program unless they *ask* me to send them there—but jail certainly is an option if that is what you choose" (Court Session, October 23, 1996).

Justice, in the view of the court, appears to require that drug court program participants be provided meaningful access to fundamental social resources—adequate education, housing, and employment—before courts can fairly treat them as criminals. By calling on the community to assist it in developing access to these resources, the court reallocates to the community some responsibility for the social inequities that undergird the low-level wrongdoing in its midst. By recognizing the social as well as the physiological realities of ongoing drug dependency, the court recasts the problem of drug offending—once a matter of individual delinquency, then a matter of individual illness—as a matter influenced, although not determined, by social circumstances. By expanding to include nondivertable drug offenders in a related drug court program, the court continues to redefine the line beyond which one becomes simply criminal. Finally, in elaborating a symbolic contractual relationship with program participants, the court effectively reaffirms a social compact between the lawful community and those on law's margins.

Conclusion

The reason for establishing a treatment drug court in Oakland was not much different from the impetus elsewhere. The shape the early drug court took, however, was clearly a consequence of the limited resources Oakland had available for a drug court program.

Two things in particular stand out about the Oakland drug court: the fact that it was established at all, given the low level of interest and support at the outset, and the difference it has managed to make with notably limited resources. From a program with admirable but modest goals—reducing the time low-level drug offenders spend in the criminal justice system by offering them access to and incentives for following through on a collection of treatment services—it has become a program that is rethinking whether and when a court should consider a drug offender criminal and thus subject to punishment. Not—the court is clear about this—that people don't bear some responsibility for the poor choices they make, but rather that it is unjust to hold them fully and individually responsible when they have had restricted access to fundamental social resources.

Because other social institutions are failing, however, the court finds itself in the position of having to provide access to social resources as the condition on which it can administer justice. Whether the court, as it develops its ability to provide program participants with access to social resources, will want to limit this access to offenders is one question that Oakland faces. How one should feel about the court as the central point of access to fundamental social resources for the disadvantaged segment of the community is another. Such an arrangement suggests further social division between the "haves" who can access resources freely, as it were, and the "have-nots" who access resources only or primarily through the intervention of the court.

As Judge Harbin-Forte (personal interview, November 27, 1996) observes, the emergence of the court as the doorway to the community's access to services is "historically ironic, particularly for African Americans, because traditionally the court has been a place where African Americans have had their rights taken away. It is widely perceived as the place where injustice is done—not justice." She believes, however, that the court sends an important message to the community about what constitutes justice and about the court itself as a community-serving, not community-oppressing, institution when it orchestrates the investment of resources in those whose social disadvantages may undergird their drug dependency. Whether the court will be able to tap into resources sufficient to the vital tasks at hand—and be able to deliver justice as it is coming to understand that concept—remains to be seen.

Notes

1. Even separately, these programs—each of which admits about 1,000 participants annually—are among the nation's largest.

2. AR Associates report that 9 of 51 African American judges statewide sit on the Oakland Municipal Court bench, but, in fact, 3 of these 9 are court commissioners. It may be that those counted as municipal court judges elsewhere in California are also commissioners, not judges; so even 48 may be an overcount. And, of course, these numbers shift from year to year.

3. Indeed, of 88 municipal courts statewide, only 2 have an African American majority on the bench: Compton Municipal Court (where African Americans are 10 of 14 judges or 71.4%) and Inglewood Municipal Court (where 6 of 7 judges—85.7%—are African American).

4. According to the Commission on the Future of the California Courts (1993), the gross disparity between the racial composition of the bench and bar and the racial composition of the population "create[s] the impression of a justice system run by and for white Californians" (p. 75).

5. The bill seeking this funding was Assembly Bill 248, proposed by then-Oakland Assemblyman and later Oakland mayor Elihu Harris.

6. In a nutshell, drug offense arrestees found to be on probation were "849b-ed" (that is, their arrest was nullified under section 849b of the California Penal Code); immediately rearrested under a no-bail probation hold; subjected to probation revocation with a hearing, if they invoked that right, but usually without a hearing; and because the arrest was nullified, without arraignment on any new charges. See Greenspan (1991, pp. 143-146). According to Greenspan, "Part of the organizational foundation of the program . . . involved obtaining the judge's agreement that he would sentence these probationers as if they were convicted of the new offense" (p. 149).

7. Over the course of the 1980s, California's prison population more than quadrupled (from about 23,000 to about 100,000), and the jail population more than doubled (from about 30,000 to about 70,000). In fact, according to Franklin Zimring

and Gordon Hawkins (1995), "After 1985, the California system added more prisoners each *year* than the system added in the average *decade* between 1950 and 1980." They add, "The addition of 120,000 prisoners in just over a decade is without precedent in the statistical record of imprisonment in the Western world" (pp. 102-104).

8. The county defunded the JCC in 1991—just as it received a grant from the State Justice Institute for a conference that would bring together judges, treatment providers, public defenders, district attorneys, and probation officers and administrators in what Judge Peggy Hora (personal interview, December 10, 1996) has referred to as "the first interdisciplinary judicial education event in the history of California." With the support of the Administrative Office of the Courts, however, the JCC substance abuse committee managed to continue operating until the conference ("Meeting the Challenge: A Judicial Perspective on Substance Abuse and the Role of the Courts") took place in November 1992.

9. Judge Peggy Hora (personal interview, December 10, 1996)—the first woman on the bench in the San Leandro-Hayward Municipal Court when she was elected in November 1984—is an author of national sentencing guidelines for pregnant offenders, an avid proponent of drug courts, and an educator of other judges about substance abuse among criminal defendants (Daily Journal Corporation, 1996).

10. The program originally called for probation officers to prepare substantial progress reports for drug court participants by Week 8, because of arrangements internal to the Probation Department. To have time to prepare their reports, they would meet with defendants Weeks 1 and 2 of the program, but not Weeks 3 or 5, with the result that many defendants missed Week 4 as well, and the program lost much of its momentum. The court and the Probation Department consequently renegotiated, with the court agreeing to hear progress reports at Week 10 and Probation agreeing to meet with defendants weekly (Tauber, personal interview, October 27, 1996).

11. Initially, budget constraints allowed for only three random drug tests over the initial 10-week period (Tauber, 1993, p. 4). Today, participants are tested six times in 10 weeks and more frequently if the situation seems to require it, although the cost of urinalysis is a growing concern, which may result in a reduction in its use.

12. Originally, Tauber compared the first 130 divertees of each year. Subsequently, he found that some of these cases had to be eliminated, reducing the sample size to 110.

13. Establishing funding for aftercare services is currently one of the Oakland drug court's highest priorities.

14. These did no analysis of outcomes by sex or race (although they provided data on sex and race) but focused, rather, on outcomes for youthful offenders (18 to 30 years) as the most malleable segment of the drug-using population. Although the sample sizes were too small to support any statistically significant inferences, Tauber believes the data provided evidence that the program did, indeed, work best for younger offenders.

15. California Senate Bill 1369, which was approved by the Governor on September 30, 1996 and became effective as of January 1, 1997, requires a guilty plea and deferred entry of judgment as a condition of eligibility for drug diversion, but it provides that courts may continue operating drug courts as pre-guilty plea diversion programs where the District Attorney, Public Defender, and court agree to this arrangement.

16. Judge Jenkins preferred providing individualized responses to the personal predicaments faced by drug court probationers rather than signing contracts. None-

theless, the language of contract has been widely employed in the Superior Court drug court. Indeed, the metaphorical possibilities of concrete drug court elements appear to be an important source of the court's ability to grow and change.

17. "Soon you'll have your GED and get this felony matter dismissed. Good work!" Harbin-Forte told a young African American man. "Yeah, what I really need is a job," he commented. "We'll get you a job, too!" Harbin-Forte responded with enthusiasm. Harbin-Forte (1996c).

References

AR Associates. (1995). *Racial and ethnic composition of the California trial courts: A report to the judicial council advisory committee on racial and ethnic bias in the courts.* Camarillo, CA: Author.

Commission on the Future of the California Courts. (1993). *Justice in the balance: 2020.*

Daily Journal Corporation. (1996). *Northern California judicial profiles: Volume 1.* Los Angeles: Author.

General Accounting Office. (1997). *Drug courts: Overview of growth, characteristics, and results.* Washington, DC: Author.

Greenspan, R. (1991). *The transformation of criminal due process in the administrative state: The targeted urban crime narcotics task force.* Unpublished Ph.D. dissertation, University of California at Berkeley.

Midtown Community Court. (undated). *Red Hook Community Court and Justice Center.* New York: Author.

National Center for State Courts. (1996). *Oakland drug court assessment.* Denver, CO: Author.

Setterberg, F. (1986). Drugs and justice in Oakland. *California Lawyer, 6*(5), 37.

Tauber, J. S. (1993, March 10). *The importance of immediate and intensive intervention in a court-ordered drug rehabilitation program: An evaluation of the FIRST diversion project after two years.* Paper presented to the President's Commission on Model State Drug Laws.

Tauber, J. S. (1995a, January 9). *An evaluation of the Oakland drug court after three years.* Paper presented at the National Association of Drug Court Professionals National Training Conference.

Tauber, J. S. (1995b, April 14). *Oakland drug court data after four years.* Unpublished report.

U.S. Bureau of the Census. (1994) *County and city data book.* Washington, DC: Government Printing Office.

Zimring, F. E., & Hawkins, G. (1995). *Incapacitation: Penal confinement and the restraint of crime.* New York: Oxford University Press.

4. Broward County's Dedicated Drug Treatment Court: From Postadjudication to Diversion

W. Clinton Terry, III

Many drug courts were created because criminal justice practitioners had practical problems for which they sought a solution. From this perspective, the initial shape of drug courts has reflected the interests of key institutional players involved in their implementation. For instance, if court administrators noticed that their caseloads included an increasing number of drug

AUTHOR'S NOTE: I wish to thank Lisa Stolzenberg for her assistance in the preparation of this chapter and Pat Voss for proofreading and making invaluable editorial suggestions. The final content and presentation of the materials in this chapter remains, as always, the author's responsibility.

cases, which were causing delays in processing the more serious felony cases, they might have advocated the creation of specialized drug courts to handle only drug cases, as some courts have done. Similarly, court administrators might have sought the assistance of treatment providers to which these cases would be referred, in hopes of reducing the number of people returning to the court system, thus providing a longer-term solution to the drug overcrowding problem, as other courts have done. If, probation officers noticed that their caseloads had become increasingly weighted with individuals convicted of drug offenses, they might have advocated treatment for their probationers as a condition of their probation. Perhaps, they were concerned about the welfare of their probationers, or they may have thought that drug-offending probationers who received treatment would be easier to manage, thus giving the probation officers more time to spend with their other cases. A few drug courts have gotten their start in this fashion. However drug courts got their start, these courts most often reflect what is viewed as acceptable and practical at the local community level.

The design of drug courts in the United States, especially dedicated drug treatment courts like the one found in Broward County, Florida, has taken many paths, often reflecting local circumstances and political alliances. The general dedicated drug court model employed by most jurisdictions focuses on first-time drug offenders having few, if any, prior felony arrests and/or convictions and whose initiating arrest is for possession and/or purchase of illegal substances. Rather than being incarcerated, these individuals are offered entrance into a treatment program. If treatment is successfully completed, the charges against them are dropped. Although this has been the general model, other drug courts have focused upon a wider array of offenses and offenders.

The planning and development of the Broward County Drug Court involved many agencies and people. Of particular importance were the judiciary, the State Attorney's office (SAO), the Public Defenders's office, the Broward County Addiction Recovery Center (BARC), the Department of Corrections, the Divisions of Probation and Parole, the Broward County Sheriff's Office (BSO), the Broward County Commission, and the Broward County Commission on Substance Abuse. Of all these agencies, and of the myriad individuals involved in the development of Broward's drug court, perhaps the most important agency was the SAO. Even though the SAO did not initiate the idea of the drug court, its statutory role in the prosecution of criminal cases placed the office in a position to shape the organization and operation of the drug court. Although the State Attorney was not opposed to the idea of drug offenders receiving treatment, it was the office's view that Broward's drug treatment court should be a postadjudication court. This is the view that carried the day in the beginning.

On July 1, 1991, the first offenders entered the Broward County dedicated drug treatment program administered as a postadjudication court. For the next 2 years, the discussion of whether Broward's drug court would be a postadjudication or diversionary court continued; in the end, on October 1, 1993, following appellate court action and legislative changes, the Broward County Drug Court became a diversionary program under the auspices of the state's pretrial intervention provisions.

Places, People, and Drugs

Broward County, Florida, is located along the southeast coast of Florida, north of Dade County, east of Hendry and Collier counties and the Florida Everglades, and south of Palm Beach County. Within Broward County, there are 27 municipalities, the best known of which are Fort Lauderdale and Hollywood. Comprising about 1,196 square miles, more than half of which are uninhabitable Everglades conservation area, Broward County is the second most populous county within the state. According to the Bureau of Economic and Business Research at the University of Florida, the 1996 estimate of Broward's population stands at 1,392,300; 47.9% of the residents are male, and 52.0% are female. Caucasians constitute 80.4% of the total population, African Americans, 17.5%; and other racial groups, 2.1%. People of Hispanic background, of all racial groups, constitute 12.3% of the population (Floyd, 1997).

A building boom in the western areas of the county has led to an exodus of the more prosperous white residents away from downtown areas to these newer residential communities. This trend has left the close-in areas relatively stagnant in value, so that they attract a growing population of the working poor. The trend has also created a growing corridor of African American residents stretching westward from Fort Lauderdale's inner city and northward to include nearby Lauderdale Lakes, which is now 44.4% African American, and Lauderhill, which is 37% African American. A bit further to the north, the city of Pompano Beach has experienced a rapidly growing African American population—a 120% increase in the last decade—

caused in part by an influx of Haitians. In southern Broward County, the Hispanic population is increasing dramatically. Fifteen years ago, not a single Broward municipality had a Hispanic population of more than 10%. By 1990, Cooper City, Davie, Hollywood, Miramar, and Pembroke Pines had Hispanic population exceeding that percentage.

The Broward County dedicated drug treatment program officially received clients from the Broward County Drug Court on July 1, 1991. The creation of this drug court was rooted in the widespread use of drugs; an overcrowded jail; overburdened court dockets; the high economic cost of arresting, prosecuting, and warehousing substance abuse offenders; and the social costs of high crime rates.

In 1990, the year immediately prior to the start of Broward's dedicated drug court, the Florida Department of Law Enforcement (FDLE) reported 77,174 drug arrests throughout the state. About 27% of these were for sales of illegal drugs (N = 20,769);[1] 73% were for possession (N = 56,405). Statewide, 10.2% of all arrests were for drug offenses. In Broward County, there were 11,394 drug arrests in 1990; 2,277 were arrests for sales/manufacturing, and 9,117 were arrests for possession. In short, 20% of all 1990 arrests in Broward County were for drug offenses; 20% of all drug arrests were for sales/manufacturing, and 80% were for possession. Although Broward County produced the second-largest number of drug arrests in the state during 1990, it ranked first in the state for drug possession arrests per 100,000 population with 718/100,000. To a great degree, the large number of possession and use arrests reflected an aggressive posture taken by the BSO, which periodically swept the streets in search of illegal drug activities.

An examination of the 1990 figures reveals that 66.4% of the people arrested in Broward County on drug charges were arrested for cocaine, 25.4% for marijuana, 4.7% for both cocaine and marijuana, and the remainder for some other substance or combination of substances. The average age of all people arrested for drugs was 28.4 years. People arrested for marijuana-only offenses were an average age of 25.5 years, compared to 29.4 years for those people arrested for cocaine-only offenses. About 82.5% of all drug arrestees were male; 17.5% were female. The disproportionate number of males arrested for drug offenses holds up across all types of drug use. Although Caucasians and African Americans were arrested in about equal proportions (54% Caucasian and 45.8% African American), the percentage of African Americans arrested exceeded their percentage of the population by a considerable degree (45.85 vs. 15.4%).

Moreover, there was a difference in the type of drug offenses for which these racial groups were arrested. In 1990, within Broward County, two thirds (66.6%) of people arrested for marijuana-only offenses were Caucasian; 33 percent were African American. By comparison, 63.5% of persons charged with a cocaine-only offenses were African Americanm; 36.5% were Caucasian.

According to the 1990 arrest data, the primary drug of choice in Broward County was cocaine, especially crack cocaine. The Broward County Drug Court was created specifically to deal with this problem. At the outset, only people charged with possession and/or purchase of cocaine were eligible for admission. Those who had possession of cocaine for the purpose of sale or delivery were ineligible for admission.

In the Beginning—Agencies

The Seventeenth Judicial Circuit of South Florida

As with many courts, the Seventeenth Judicial Circuit Court of South Florida is organizationally divided into General Civil, Criminal, Probate, and Juvenile Divisions. The drug court and the habitual offender court, two distinct and separate courts, are part of the Criminal Division of the Court. In 1990, the number of cases entering Broward's courts was increasing. There was no specific dedicated drug treatment court, although one had been operating for about a year across Broward's southern boundary in Dade County. Informal discussions and visits to Miami's drug court, located in Dade County, Florida, were made by members of the BSO, the SAO, members of county government, BARC, and the Broward County Commission on Substance Abuse.

In January 1991, under the leadership of Judge Mark A. Speiser, Chief Administrative Judge of the Criminal Division of the Seventeenth Judicial Circuit Court, a Drug Court Task Force was formed. This task force consisted of members of the Seventeenth Judicial Circuit, the SAO, the Public Defender's office, the Clerk of the Court, the Broward County Commission on Substance Abuse, the Broward County Commission, the BSO and various other local law enforcement agencies, the Department of Corrections, the Divisions of Probation and Parole, the private bar, and the bondsmen. They met often in the jury box of Judge Speiser's Court. Eventually, they chose Judge Robert Fogan to head the drug court. Funds were obtained from the BSO, the Broward County Commission, and the Broward County Commission on Substance Abuse. A building was rented within walking distance of the courthouse, large enough to handle 1,200 people during the course of a year. BARC would provide counseling and treatment at this new location for the clients sent there by the drug court.

State Attorney's Office

The organization of the Broward County SAO mirrors the organization of the Seventeenth Judicial Circuit Court. Its County Court Division handles all misdemeanor cases; the Felony Trial Division handles all general felony cases, and the Juvenile Division handles the juvenile cases. In addition, there are specialized units handling capital offenses, economic crimes, sexual assault and child abuse offenses, domestic violence cases, and minimum/mandatory drug crimes. The State's Attorney assigned to the drug court came from the felony trial division.

No new newcomer to drug issues, the SAO had long been involved with these issues. Beginning in 1972, the SAO was instrumental in developing a Pretrial Intervention (PTI) program administered by the State Department of Corrections, Divisions of Probation and Parole. Within this program, first-time offenders committing certain crimes were ineligible. For instance, people arrested for drugs involving cocaine or heroin were excluded. However, drug offenders charged with possessing less than 1 pound of bulk marijuana (seeds and stems included), and/or 15 amphetamine or barbiturate pills were eligible. People charged with committing nonviolent, nonvice third-degree felonies were also eligible. Admission to PTI also required the consent of the victim and the arresting police officer. On successful completion of this 1-year program, the case was *nolle prosequi*.

The SAO's orientation toward Broward's PTI program reveals three basic policy concerns: (a) public safety, (b) the addictive nature of hard drugs such as heroin and cocaine, and (c) the criminal involvement of hard drug users. In short, people who use cocaine and heroin, the latter of which is used infrequently in Broward County, are often involved in additional criminal activities in support of their habit. Consequently, it was felt that people involved with hard drugs are a greater risk to the public safety than people using other forms of illegal substances.

Broward County Addiction Recovery Center

BARC is the county agency providing assistance to individuals and their families experiencing alcohol and/or other drug-related problems. In the years prior to the advent of the drug court, the demand for indigent services allowed BARC little opportunity to work with criminal justice clients. Toward the end of the 1980s, however, BARC, directed by Marie Reynolds, was instrumental in creating Alternative Treatment Against Crack Cocaine. During this time, Fort Lauderdale had a 100-bed municipal jail, referred to as the "Hooker Hilton," which had a few empty beds. The Fort Lauderdale Police Department approached BARC with the suggestion that it offer a treatment program inside their jail. Funded by the county, the jail set aside 20 beds for this purpose. Offenders sent to this jail could sign up for the 90-day drug treatment program. Although charges were not dropped upon completion of the program and although no data about program outcomes were collected, the program was considered successful and is still in operation today.

Shortly after BARC began working with drug offenders at the Fort Lauderdale Municipal Jail, it received funding from Judge William Hoeveler of the U.S. District Court for the Southern District of Florida to provide outpatient treatment for substance abuse offenders referred to it by the courts. The situation was this: The Broward County Jail had been under a federal order not to exceed the number of inmates for which the facility had been designed. Exceeding this cap, which occurred regularly, resulted in a $1,000 fine for each day it was exceeded. From this money, Judge Hoeveler was able to fund an intensive outpatient treatment program. Under this program, people came in for counseling 3 days a week for 90 days. BARC learned from this program that a criminal population needed separate treatment, focusing on the criminal consequences of their addiction. This program became the proving ground for what occurred in the Broward County dedicated drug court treatment program.

Broward County Commission

The Broward County Commission consists of seven elected officials. As with county government everywhere, the commission is responsible for creating, monitoring, and funding a wide range of county services. Within the area of criminal justice, it funds the BSO, certain functions of the court (e.g., bailiffs and court reporting), and the jail.

In the spring of 1991, the commission was asked to enter into a partnership with other county agencies for the purpose of starting a drug court. The BSO would pay part of the cost; another part would be paid by the Broward County Commission on Substance Abuse in the form of a grant; part would be paid by using Judge Hoeveler's jail fine money; and the remainder of the funding would be provided by the Broward County Commission. Because the county was being asked to fund only 3 months of drug court activities for that fiscal year, and because there were a number of community groups entering into this partnership, each sharing in the success and/or failure of the venture, the county commission had little difficulty embracing the proposal. Although the initial proposal spread the costs of the drug court among several agencies, it is now funded 100% by county property taxes.

In part, the commission's role in the development of Broward County's drug court was tied to the purse strings it held. Nevertheless, the commission had a long involvement with substance abuse issues, and it was through the voice of Commissioner John Hart that the commission gave its strong support to the drug court. From among the county commission's staff, Pete Corwin took the lead role in attending most organizational meetings where the development of the drug court was discussed, thus providing a link between the commission, agencies, and other community groups and members. The commission was and still is the major source of funding for BARC, and through BARC's work, the commission was involved with most county substance abuse programs. The county had also received several federal grants for treatment programs 1 to 2 years prior to the implementation of the drug court. In addition, the commission was concerned about the overcrowded jail; consequently, it was interested in the drug court as a means of helping solve this problem.

Broward Sheriff's Office

The Sheriff of Broward County during 1991 was Nick Navarro. High on his enforcement agenda were the state's drug laws. He conducted numerous street sweeps, buy busts, and other sting operations resulting in the arrest of numerous drug offenders. He and his staff were also involved in several funded programs that helped lay the groundwork for the development of Broward's drug court.

During June 1990, the BSO proposed to enter into a project it labeled Operation Second Chance, for which it received a grant from the Department of Community Affairs in Tallahassee, Florida. Initially, this project was to take first-time drug offenders who had been arrested for purchasing cocaine within 1,000 feet of public school properties, thus facing a minimum/mandatory 3-year sentence, and offer them a second chance in the form of a 1-year supervised treatment and rehabilitation program. The original idea was later revised to include both possession and purchase of cocaine, without regard to their proximity to public schools. A human services coordinator, special projects coordinator, and three substance abuse specialists were hired. As a consequence, this project evolved into a demonstration effort for first-time drug offenders placed into a treatment program and was eventually merged into the developing Broward County drug court.

The Broward Commission on Substance Abuse

The Broward County Commission on Substance Abuse, directed by David Choate, was created by the United Way of Broward County in 1988 and was responsible for receiving, distributing, and monitoring federal anti-drug abuse money.[2] Its membership included 113 community leaders and its mission was

> To initiate, encourage and coordinate a comprehensive community-wide effort to combat illegal drugs and their harmful effects on individuals and society; to raise public awareness of the drug and alcohol problem; to help evaluate existing and planned anti-drug efforts; and to advocate for needed changes, modifications and additions to the service delivery system as they relate to drug abuse. (The Broward County Commission on Substance Abuse, 1993)

To accomplish these goals, seven task forces were created. These task forces encompassed the areas of treatment, law enforcement/criminal justice, prevention/education, drug-free workplace, religion, media/public awareness, and the Legislature. They operated under the auspices of the Broward County Commission on Substance Abuse. These task forces provided a vehicle for discussing substance abuse issues in Broward County. As an agency within the Broward County United Way, the Commission on Substance Abuse was viewed as a neutral, nonpolitical entity, and as such, it was able to bring many diverse interests to the planning table. During the latter part of

1990, the Broward Commission on Substance Abuse also became interested in helping establish a drug court. Not only did this fit within its strategic plan, but it also provided an issue of interest to a number of task forces, bringing many of them closer together.

Difference in Points of View

During the planning process of the Broward County Drug Court, many differences between individuals and agencies were expressed. There was, however, general agreement about the need for treatment. The most important difference revolved around whether the Broward County Drug Court should be a diversionary or postadjudication program. As a diversionary program, it would fall under Florida's PTI statute (Florida Statute 948.08), allowing for the preadjudication deferral of prosecution and dismissal of charges on the successful completion of treatment.[3] In a postadjudication court, people would plead guilty or no contest to the possession and/or purchase charges against them. A 1-year sentence to probation would be given, with the stipulation that offenders complete the drug treatment program. On the successful completion of the treatment program, the court records could be expunged.

The differences between the SAO, the judiciary, and others were a reflection of the differences in perspective between criminal justice and treatment orientations. From a criminal justice perspective, the role of the state is to protect the community from criminal offenses. This is accomplished by arresting, prosecuting, and punishing offenders. It is hoped that the penalties administered will deter offenders from future offenses.

The issue here is public safety. Because the SAO, as the result of their long involvement with the PTI program, had maintained that cocaine users were a more serious threat to the public safety than other types of drug users, the office felt compelled, as a agent of the state, to do what it could to ensure the public safety. In this case, the State Attorney argued for a postadjudication drug treatment court. This would keep people under the supervision of the state through the Department of Probation and Parole, which, it was thought would help ensure conforming behavior. In addition, it was felt that the threat of being charged with a probation violation for failure to meet its conditions and thus possibly being sent to prison would also restrain people from committing any additional offenses.

The SAO was criticized for its stand on how to deal with cocaine offenders. As Ralph Ray from the SAO stated in a discussion with this author, "We used to be accused of being against the drug court. We were never against it, but we felt that you needed to weigh the public interest with the individual interest of these people who had violated the law."

From a treatment perspective, substances abusers suffer a life-long illness from which they are continually recovering. Along the way, it is assumed that relapses will occur, not from a willful refusal to exercise conforming behavior, but from the conditions associated with addiction. Responses to these relapses may be handled with firmness, but they require understanding of the conditions out of which they arise. To sanction an individual for relapsing, thus calling public attention to this failure, may have the undesirable effect of reinforcing rather than extinguishing the behavior. Such recognition may be viewed positively. And if it is viewed negatively, it may further damage a person's self-esteem and self-worth, thus promoting further drug use as an escape. From this perspective, handling relapses and associated behaviors, including technical violations of probation, is a much more complicated matter than the simple application of sanctions to rule violations.

Whereas the SAO argued for greater supervision, those favoring the view that recovery was a long-term process filled with many pitfalls and failures argued for more tolerance and incentives. What was needed, they thought, was not stricter supervision and the threat of punishment but clearly defined inducements, support, and understanding for the problems confronting the struggling substance abuser. What greater incentive could there be than the dismissal of criminal charges on the successful completion of the treatment program?

In the end, the views of the SAO prevailed, and the Broward County Drug Court became a postadjudication court. This lasted from July 1, 1991 to October 31, 1993.

From Postadjudication to Diversion

The issue of whether Broward's drug court should be changed to a diversionary court was a topic of much discussion, particularly toward the end of the first year, when participants began asking questions about having their records expunged after graduation from the program. Obviously, people who had successfully completed the program wanted their charges dismissed. Unfortunately, no formal agreement had been reached with them concerning the subsequent dismissal of their charges.

It became apparent that the federal government treated no contest pleas, as well as adjudication withheld, as guilty pleas. Consequently, people who were not U.S. citizens could be deported for having been convicted of a felony. People who were citizens would mostly likely be denied federal employment. Within the state of Florida, it also became apparent that people pleading guilty would not be eligible for some state jobs. Finally, it also became known that expunged records, which required the defendant to petition the court, did not completely destroy the record. Expunged records could still be uncovered by law enforcement and other government agencies.

This issue came to a head when Judge Fogan, exercising his statutory authority, dismissed the charges of some of the offenders who had successfully completed the treatment program. To do this, he withdrew their original plea, thus allowing him to dismiss the charges. The SAO took exception to these actions and appealed his decision in two cases to the Fourth District Court of Appeals in Florida. The court upheld Judge Fogan's decision (*State v. Dugan,* 1995).

At the same time, efforts were made to clarify Florida Statute 397.12, under which Judge Fogan had dismissed the charges of the drug court defendants. According to the original statute, if a judge required a defendant to participate in a state-licensed treatment program, this "referral may be *in lieu of* or in addition to final adjudication, imposition of a penalty or sentence, or any other similar action" (Florida Statute 397.12). This paragraph was repealed and replaced with Florida Statute 397.705, which reads in part: "If referred by the court, the referral may be *instead of* or in addition to final adjudication, imposition of penalty or sentence, or other action." In addition, Florida Statute 948.08(6)(2), which spells out the conditions of Florida's PTI program, was changed to read, "The court shall dismiss the charges upon the finding that the defendant has successfully completed the pretrial intervention program." In short, drug court judges in the State of Florida now have the clear authority to dismiss charges against drug defendants after they had completed a drug treatment program to which the drug court judge had referred them. These new statutes went into effect on October 1, 1993, at which time the Broward County Drug Court officially became a diversionary court.

Broward County Drug Court as a Postadjudication Model

Broward County's drug court was modeled after the Miami Drug Court, replete with the use of acupuncture. The major difference in the beginning was that the Broward County Drug Court was a postadjudication court, whereas the Miami court was a diversion court built on a pretrial intervention model.

Program Eligibility

The focus of the Broward County's drug court was initially on cocaine and crack-cocaine offenders. To be eligible for admission into treatment, a defendant had to be arrested for the purchase and/or possession of cocaine. In addition, defendants had to be first-time felony offenders. If they had a prior felony conviction or conviction resulting in PTI or probation, they were ineligible. If they were accused of additional felony charges at the time of their possession and/or purchase arrest, they were ineligible. People eligible for treatment had to be 18 years of age or older and residents of Broward County. In addition to these judicial requirements, BARC required that eligible clients be free from any medical problems that would prohibit active participation in treatment, able to maintain themselves in a nonresidential program, and not suicidal, psychotic, severely depressed, or prone to violence.[4]

About 9 months after the first person entered Broward County's drug court, the eligibility requirements were expanded.[5] After March 31, 1992, if a person had committed an offense more than 10 years prior to the current arrest for possession and/or purchase of cocaine and if he or she had been free from state supervision for a period of 10 years, he or she would be eligible for entry into drug court. The following people would also be eligible:

- Any person charged with tampering with evidence in which the evidence involved no more than three rocks of cocaine

- Any person charged with possession and/or purchase of barbiturates or amphetamines of no more than 15 pills
- Any person charged with possession and/or purchase of marijuana not exceeding one pound

From Arrest to Treatment

Because Broward had a postadjudication court, people arrested for possession and/or purchase of cocaine were examined by the BSO's Pretrial Services to determine program eligibility, generally within 24 hours of arrest. It was the consensus of the Drug Court Task Force that people arrested for drug offenses should appear as soon as possible before the drug court judge because they were more likely to accept treatment during this period of crisis.

Upon indicating a desire to receive treatment, the defendants were sent to the BARC treatment facility, either immediately or within several days. The delay depended on whether the judge sent the person back to jail for a few days to "sober up." The BSO transported these individuals from the jail to the drug court treatment facility, along with accompanying paperwork, and turned them over to treatment personnel for processing.

At arraignment, generally 21 days after arrest, offenders again appeared before the drug court judge. If they pled guilty or no contest to the charges against them, they were sentenced to probation for 1 year. At this time, they were officially admitted to the Broward County Drug Court. Through different legal maneuvering, certain defendants were able to remain in drug court for long periods of time while their cases were adjudicated. Some of these individuals were able to have their cases dismissed only to find themselves ineligible for drug court because, technically, they were no longer the subject of violating any state drug laws.

People entering the drug court promised to fulfill the conditions of the treatment program. They were also required to appear at the probation department each month and to fulfill all the conditions established by the Department of Corrections, Probation and Parole Services. In short, they were required to report to their probation officer and to make numerous visits to the Broward County dedicated drug-treatment program facility. Defendants had to go to the treatment facility daily during the first 3 weeks and three times a week during the next 23 weeks. Fulfilling these conditions was a much stiffer sentence than the 2 years of regular probation received by most first-time drug offenders and did not entail any visits to a treatment facility nor participation in the treatment's frequent drug-screening program.

Program Phases

Broward's drug court was originally designed as a three-phase program that incorporated group and individual therapy, fellowship meetings, case staffings, urinalysis, and acupuncture. Phase I lasted 3 weeks (15 days) and was the most intensive segment of the treatment program. The focus was on detoxification and adaptation to the treatment setting. Urine testing was done five times each week. Two group therapy sessions per week, five fellowship meetings per week, and one individual session per week were also required during Phase I. Fifteen (15) acupuncture sessions were available, if chosen by the participant. Clients who successfully completed Phase I were allowed to move into Phase II on the recommendation of the court liaison to the judge (Alcohol and Drug Abuse Services Division, 1991, pp. 2, 4).

Phase II was a 23-week program emphasizing a drug-free lifestyle, social adjustment, and the development of appropriate mechanisms for coping with stressful situations. The weekly requirements were attendance at one group therapy session, one fellowship meeting per week, three urine tests, attendance at individual therapy sessions according to the treatment plan developed during Phase I, and adherence to the recommendations of the resource person responsible for planning, developing, and implementing an educational/vocational program for the client. Six weeks into Phase II, clients who had successfully completed program requirements up to that point were eligible for early movement into Phase III if they had accomplished the following: stable housing arrangements, stable work situation, consistently clean urine, and a healthy support system (Alcohol and Drug Abuse Services Division, 1991, pp. 4-7).

Phase III was the final segment of treatment. The emphasis during this program phase was on education and work skills. However, clients were still required to attend one group session and one fellowship meeting per week, as well as individual sessions on request of the primary counselor. To successfully complete Phase III and graduate from the drug court, clients had to have clean urine, be actively working, be enrolled in vocational rehabilitation or on the job training, and have completed all group, fellowship, and individual sessions (Alcohol and Drug Abuse Services Division, 1991, p. 9).

Broward County Drug Court as a Diversion Court

On October 1, 1993, the Broward County Drug Court became a diversionary court. People participating in the drug court are now placed in Broward County's PTI program, and prosecution is deferred; no one pleads guilty or no contest, and the judge dismisses charges on successful completion of PTI and treatment. There is also a new drug court judge, Judge Melanie G. May.

The drug court now handles all second- or third-degree drug felonies involving the possession and/or purchase of any controlled substance as defined by Florida Statute 893.03.[6] As with any felony arrest, individuals arrested for purchase or possession of a controlled substance are randomly assigned to one of the regular criminal divisions. Pretrial Services still conducts daily preliminary assessments of offender eligibility. Those found eligible and interested in treatment may be released from custody to treatment. Because this is done daily, offenders may find themselves in treatment soon after their arrest, thus preserving the general principle that sooner is better when it comes to the commencement of treatment.

After the preliminary assessment of eligibility, Pretrial Services turns over to the Department of Corrections the list of people found eligible for drug court; the department then completes a thorough criminal background check of each individual within 24 hours. Those verified to be eligible are transferred from the criminal division to which they were initially assigned into the drug court division of the court.

At arraignment, the Department of Corrections provides the defendant with a deferred prosecution agreement to sign. Defendants then apply for admission into PTI and undergo an initial interview. Those who have not participated in treatment prior to their arraignment are often given a 2-week continuance to decide whether they want to participate in treatment. Those defendants who decide not to participate are transferred back to the criminal division to which they were originally assigned.

Completion of the program requires attendance for a period of 1 year at the treatment facility, as well as compliance with all the rules and regulations of the drug court division judge, the treatment facility, and the Department of Corrections, which administers the PTI program. In determining an offender's successful completion of the program, the drug court judge considers the recommendation coming from the county's treatment providers and from the PTI administrators. When offenders successfully complete treatment, the drug court judge dismisses the charges against them.

The direction of the treatment program remains relatively the same. The focus remains on developing a treatment plan for each person entering the program and providing them with individual and group counseling. There are now four phases rather than three. The first phase is the BP Phase, which occurs prior to arraignment and lasts for about a month. During this phase, the defendant (i.e., client) is evaluated, receives individual counseling, and participates in group sessions. This phase provides an opportunity for defendants to be evaluated and, in turn, allows the defendants time to form an opinion about whether the program would benefit them and whether they want to participate in it. Those individuals participating in the BP Phase will have a pretty good idea about the program and its expectations when the judge, at arraignment, asks them whether they want to participate in the treatment program. Phase I, following the BP Phase, lasts for another month, Phase II lasts for 4 months, and Phase III last for about 6 months. The goals of these last three phases are similar to those of the original treatment plan. Urine testing is now done randomly, even though more urine tests are taken during the BP and Phase I periods. Acupuncture remains available and is still considered an important part of the program, especially during the first several months.

Program Assessment

There is, unfortunately, no data by which a comparison of the postadjudication and diversionary courts can be undertaken.[7] There is, however, considerable information available about individuals who went through the treatment program during its first year. Whether these people are substantially different from the subsequent graduates of the court cannot be answered without additional data. However, the following is worth considering. First, the eligibility requirements have changed little over the years. Although a wider range of illegal substances is allowed, the focus is still on possession or purchase of illegal substances. People charged with delivery or sales are still ineligible. Second, although the people admitted during the first year of treatment were charged, for the most part, with the possession or purchase of cocaine, a large percentage of these individuals had used several other illegal substances during the 90-day period prior to their initiating arrest, not to mention the wide use of alcohol. Third, the basic structure of the treatment program has changed a little, yet remains very similar to the original program. Hence, it is likely that the people being treated today are also very similar to those treated during the first year. Whether there are, in fact, differences between the first-year cohort and current drug court participants will have to be determined by future research.

What follows is a description of the people entering the first year of Broward's treatment program (1991-1992) along with a report of the ongoing evaluation of these individuals compared to a group of people who met the eligibility criteria but declined the court's offer to receive treatment, thus receiving regular probation instead.

Client Profile

During the initial planning stages of the Broward County Drug Court, a decision was made to collect information on the people receiving treatment during the first year of program operation and then to follow these individuals for a period of 1 year after graduation. The following client profile is based on a diagnostic questionnaire completed by each individual on entrance into the program.

Of the first-time drug offenders entering the Drug Treatment Program, 49.7% were Caucasian, 44.2% were African American; 4.8% were Hispanic, and the remainder were either Native American or Asian. Compared to the demographic composition of Broward County, African Americans were overrepresented (15.4% versus 44.2%).

The average age of people entering Broward's dedicated drug court program was 30.5 years. Almost half of this population was between the ages of 26 and 35. This suggest that the entrants into the Broward's dedicated drug court treatment program were slightly older than the average age of 29.4 years for people arrested in Broward County for cocaine offenses (Terry, Rogers, & Tomchik, 1992).

About 5.5% of people entering treatment had completed elementary or middle school only; 35.8% had completed some high school, 42.1% graduated from high school; 12.7% completed some college; 3.4% graduated from college, and .5% had completed some post-collegiate work. Of those completing high school, 11.3% had received GED degrees, and 22.3% had attended at least some vocational school. No one who had not graduated from high school was currently enrolled in school, nor was anyone preparing their GED or attending vocational school.

About 11% of first-time drug offenders entering Broward's dedicated drug treatment program were married; 10% were separated, 18% were divorced, and .5 percent were widowed. Surprisingly, slightly more than 60% had never been married. Although this suggests that 89% of this population were living alone at the time of the intake interview, about 80% of participants said they were living with someone else, irrespective of their marital status. About half (47.8%) of these people had been living with someone else for longer than a year, and 41.4% had been living with someone else for less than 6 months.[8] About 78.4% reported having no dependents.

On entrance into Broward's dedicated drug treatment program, 50.7% indicated they were currently employed; 49.3% were currently unemployed. Of those currently working, 26.7% were working less than 40 hours a week; 50.4% were working 40 hours a week, and 22.6% were working more than 40 hours a week. Their average annual employment was 24.8 weeks.[9]

What appears from this client profile is the description of a group of people living on the margins of society. Many of those entering Broward's drug court were unattached, having never been married or being separated, divorced, or widowed. The vast majority had no dependents nor had anyone counting on them for support. Many had not lived at their present location for a very long period of time. Their educational levels were relatively low. At their time of admission into treatment, very few people were involved in efforts that would improve their educational credentials. Employment histories were somewhat spotty. Many had not been working full-time for any length of time, and many were unskilled.

Drug Use

The drugs of choice for those entering Broward County's dedicated drug treatment program during its first year were alcohol, marijuana, and cocaine. In discussing cocaine, a distinction between powder and crack cocaine should be made. When asked whether they used cocaine during the past 90 days, about 25% of the respondents indicated that they had used cocaine during this period of time. What the respondents understood by this question was a reference to powder cocaine. When asked the same question about crack cocaine, about 52% said they had used crack during the past 90 days. The level of usage was different. Of those using powder cocaine, 39% indicated that they used it more than twice a week, whereas about 63% of the crack users used crack more than twice a week. Only 5.5% of the powder cocaine users used it every day for the past 90 days, compared to 23.7% of crack users. Patterns of usage also differed. Crack users were less likely to use powder cocaine than powder users would be to use crack. Nevertheless, each group tended to avoid the others' type of cocaine use.

Almost half (47.2%) of the people entering Broward County's dedicated drug treatment program during its first year used marijuana. Of these individuals, about 57% used marijuana two or more times weekly during the 90 days prior to admission. Almost 19% used it daily. Obviously, marijuana is the second drug of choice among those individuals entering treatment, even prior to it being formally allowed into the program during March 1992.

About 78.5% of Broward's dedicated drug court treatment program participants used alcohol during the 90 days prior to their admission. Of these people, almost 30% used it daily, about 43% used it two or more times a week, and 28% used it once a week or less than once a week. In short, alcohol and cocaine were often used together. Cocaine acted as an upper, whereas alcohol acted as a downer. In informal discussions with these respondents, some of them commented that they turned to cocaine to escape their alcoholism.

Other drug choices were too infrequent to report. By way of summary, they were as follows: 27 people reported taking downers (pills), 13 admitted taking opiates, 11 took uppers (pills), 11 used cocaine intravenously, 8 reported taking hallucinogens, 4 people took heroin intravenously, 4 people used "ice"—crystal or methedrine, 1 person used inhalants, and 1 person used basuco.

Program Graduation and Failure to Complete Treatment

Ideally, each person entering Broward County's dedicated drug treatment program should have graduated within 1 year of admission, coinciding with the 1 year of probation to which they were sentenced. Thus, the last person should have left the program June 30, 1993. However, this is a population of drug offenders; therefore, there were relapses and other difficulties resulting in the extension of their probation. Of the 788 people admitted into Broward County's dedicated drug treatment court during its first year of operation, 307 people (39%) graduated from the program. What happened to the rest? About 20.7%, or 163, were nolle prosequi: No information was filed. The remainder did not complete the program for a variety of reasons. Many were dropped because their background investigations indicated they no longer met the eligibility criteria. A number elected to go to trial or take regular probation rather than to undergo the more rigorous treatment program. There were still others who were removed from the program for different reasons, sometimes behavioral in nature.

Program Evaluation

There are many questions attached to measuring the success or failure of a drug treatment program. Clearly, a primary measure of drug treatment success is whether people get clean and stay sober. However, within the context of a treatment program sponsored and funded by a local community and guided by the dictates of a judicial system, an equally compelling measure of program success is whether the subsequent criminal activities of those people receiving treatment decrease compared to similar people receiving no treatment: whether there is an overall increase in the public safety.

Quasi-Experimental Control Group

The best research design to measure program outcomes is an experimental design. Such a design would randomly assign individuals to a drug treatment program or to some other type of program. However, this was not possible in Broward County because policy makers were uncomfortable with denying treatment to people who wanted it. For this study, the closest alternative to a pure experimental group was a quasi-experimental (i.e., comparison) control group. The individuals in this group met the eligibility criteria of the drug court but decided not to participate in Broward's dedicated drug treatment program.

To identify the comparison group used, the Broward County Clerk's office compiled a list of people arrested for the purchase and/or possession of cocaine within Broward County from July 1, 1991, through June 30, 1992. This list was then randomly ordered. The people on it were examined for eligibility by the same Pre-trial Services who determined the eligibility of people who actually entered the drug treatment program during the first year, using the same criteria as were used for the first year's cohort. When a group of 300 people were identified, after examining more than 1,500 people, the search for a comparison group stopped. By comparing treatment graduates with these 300 individuals, it is possible to state with some certainty that the differences between these groups were the result of the treatment program.

A Few Data Observations

The primary focus of this outcome evaluation was rearrests. Recidivism was measured for a time period of 1 year after graduation from the treatment program for the experimental group and/or 1 year after release from probation, in the case of the comparison group. Of the 307 people who graduated from the treatment program,[10] 1 year of recidivism data was available for only 230 individuals. Of the 300 people in the comparison group, 1 year of recidivism data was available for only 73 people.[11] The following analysis is therefore based on 230 program graduates and 73 individuals who completed their probation, for a total of 303 individuals.

Recidivism for this analysis was measured four ways. First, recidivism was measured by whether a person was rearrested for any misdemeanor or felony offense. Only the initial arrest during the follow-up period was examined. Second, the initial arrests for felonies were examined separately. Third, only the initial drug rearrests during the follow-up period for drug offenses were examined. All the drug rearrests were for felonies, almost exclusively arrests for possession or purchase of an illegal substance—usually cocaine. There was only one initial misdemeanor drug rearrest during this period of time.

Recidivism was also measured in terms of the length of time that elapsed before a person committed a new offense. This was the fourth measure of recidivism, the time to failure. This measure is widely used as an indicator of the length of time a community is "safe" from the criminal acts of people being released into the community. Granted, it would be preferable if no future criminal acts were committed; however, from a policy perspective, if people commit additional offenses, it would better to support a program demonstrating longer times to failure.

Comparison Between Groups

The 230 people who graduated from Broward's dedicated drug treatment court and the 73 people from the comparison group who completed their probation were matched on the eligibility criteria for admission into the drug court. In addition, they compared well on traditional demographic variables, as may be seen in Table 4.1. For instance, the average age at admission for treatment graduates was 31.44 years, compared to 28.96 years for the comparison group. About 68% of the treatment graduates were Caucasian versus 69% for the comparison group. In contrast to these close similarities, 81% of the treatment graduates were male, compared to 68% of the probation comparison group, and there was a wider difference between the average number of days a person was in treatment compared to the number of days a person was on probation. The treatment graduates were in treatment for an average of 402.90 days, compared to 306.75 on probation for those in the comparison group.

These intergroup comparisons seem close enough, intuitively, and with the exception of age, do not produce any significant differences between these groups on the outcome measures used. There is one possible difference between these groups that deserves mention. One of the reasons some individuals chose to participate in treatment, whereas others did not, relates to their motivational state. Perhaps, the people entering treatment are mentally ready for treatment, whereas those who abstained from treatment were not ready. This might account for the differences between these groups, but it cannot be measured within the scope of this study.

Rearrests

About 19% of the treatment graduates were rearrested for either a misdemeanor or felony offense, compared to 28% of the probation comparison group, as may be seen in the column of Figure 4.1 labeled Rearrest (any rearrest). For the treatment graduates, 22 of these first rearrests were for felonies, and 19 were for misdemeanors. Of these misdemeanor arrests, six were driving under the influence (DUI) arrests.[12] For the probation releasees, 15 of their rearrests were for felonies; 4 were for misdemeanors—none of which were DUIs.

When only felony rearrests were examined, 10% of the treatment graduates and 22% of probation releasees were rearrested.[13] In other words, slightly more than twice as many probation releasees were arrested for a felony as their initial arrest than were treatment graduates. In addition, this comparison of felony arrests reveals that treatment graduates were almost as likely to be arrested for a

TABLE 4.1 Variables: Coding, Means, and Standard Deviations by Type of Program

		Drug Court (N = 221)		*Probation (N = 69)*	
Variable	*Coding Format*	*Percentage*	*SD*	*Percentage*	*SD*
Rearrest	0 = no, 1 = yes	.19	.39	.28	.45
Felony rearrest	0 = no, 1 = yes	.10	.30	.22	.42
Drug rearrest	0 = no, 1 = yes	.05	.22	.17	.38
Time to failure, all rearrests	Interval	171.39	100.75	211.00	113.70
Time to failure, felonies	Interval	171.55	106.25	183.27	106.92
Age	Interval	31.44	7.84	29.96	6.67
Gender	0 = male, 1 = female	.19	.39	.32	.47
Race	0 = white, 1 = African American	.32	.47	.31	.47
Time in program	Interval	402.90	63.18	306.13	162.59

NOTE: Type of program was coded as 1 if a defendant was released from the drug court; otherwise, coded as 0. Time to failure levels are based on the number of defendants rearrested during the 12-month follow-up period (41 in drug court and 19 in probation for any rearrest, and 22 in drug court and 15 in probation for felony rearrest).

misdemeanor offense as for a felony offense. About 19% of the drug treatment graduates were arrested for any offense (felonies and misdemeanors), and 10% were arrested for felonies. The same comparison for probation releasees was 28% for any arrest and 22% for felony arrests; hence, probation releasees are far more likely than treatment graduates to be arrested for a felony than for a misdemeanor.

When only drug rearrests were examined, there is a large difference between the treatment graduates and those individuals released from probation. Again, referring to Figure 4.1, 5% of the treatment graduates were rearrested for a drug offense within 1 year of their graduation, compared to 17% of those individuals released from probation after 1 year.

Time to Failure

As seen in Table 4.1 above, the average time to failure (i.e., rearrest for any offense) for treatment graduates was 171.39 days, compared to 211 days for those people released from probation.[14] The average

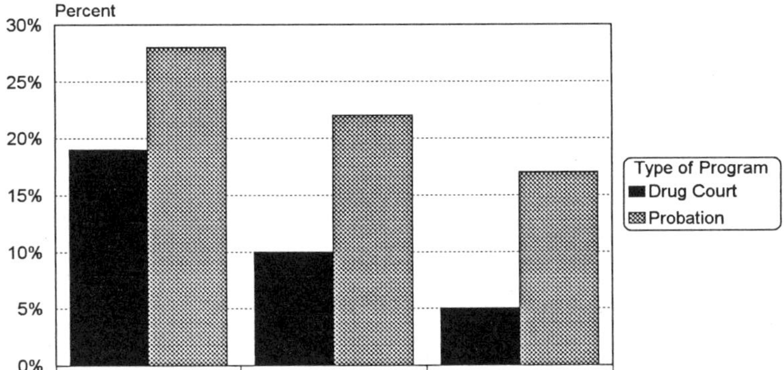

	Rearrest	Felony Rearrest	Drug Rearrest
Drug Court	19%	10%	5%
Probation	28%	22%	17%

Figure 4.1. Rearrest, Felony Rearrest, and Drug Rearrest by Drug Court and Probation

NOTE: Recidivism rates are based on the total number of defendants released from the drug court (N = 221) and from progration (N = 69).

time to failure for felony arrests was 171.55 days for treatment graduates and 183.27 days for people completing a probation program.[15] It would appear, therefore, that it took the probation comparison group a bit longer than the treatment graduates to be arrested for the first time after leaving their program. These time to failure differences were, however, statistically insignificant.

Logistic and Ordinary Least Squares Regression

Logistic and ordinary least squares (OLS) regressions were conducted on the variables of this analysis to control for the influence of other variables on the dependent variable, rearrest. Four different models were employed. The first three were logistic models; the fourth was an OLS model. The dichotomous dependent variable in the first model was rearrest for any offense; in the second model, the dependent variable was rearrest for a felony; in the third model, it was rearrest for a drug infraction; and in the fourth, which employs an ordinary least squares model, the dependent variable was

TABLE 4.2 Logistic Regression Results Predicting Rearrest, Felony Rearrest, and Drug Rearrest ($N = 290$)

	Rearrest		*Felony Rearrest*		*Drug Rearrest*	
Variable	*b*	*se*	*b*	*se*	*b*	*se*
Type of program	–.431	.379	–.889*	.426	–1.145*	.517
Age	–.087*	.024	–.071*	.029	–.054	.035
Gender	–.454	.386	–.408	.464	–.058	.519
Race	.302	.323	.253	.393	.108	.488
Time in program	–.001	.002	.001	.002	–.002	.002
Constant	1.682	.922	.728	1.080	.6201	.269

*$p < .05$ (one-tailed test).

length of time to rearrest. The first three of these regression analyses are presented in Table 4.2 above. The fourth regression model produced no statistically significant results; consequently, its findings were discussed descriptively in the previous section on time to failure.

Age at admission, seen in Table 4.2, was significantly related to rearrest for any offense and arrest for a felony, but not for drug rearrests. Younger people were more likely than older people to be rearrested. This may also account for some of the difference in felony and drug rearrests between the treatment and probation groups inasmuch as the probation group is somewhat younger than the treatment group. Age may also be related to motivation for change, which, as previously mentioned, is beyond the scope of this analysis.

Of particular importance to this analysis was the statistically significant difference between the drug rearrests of the treatment graduates and the comparison group seen in Table 4.2. Although there was no statistically significant difference between the overall rearrests of the treatment graduates and probation releasees, people from the treatment program were significantly less likely to be rearrested for either a felony or for a drug offense. This again pointed out the importance of misdemeanor offenses in their rearrests. Because these differences were statistically significant, it suggests that the treatment program has accomplished its main goals, namely, reducing the level of criminality of its graduates, compared to those offenders who received no treatment. This is also good news for treatment inasmuch as these relationships also suggest that more treatment graduates may be staying clean and sober compared to those who received no treatment.

Conclusion

The Broward County Drug Court grew out of a community need to deal with a growing crack cocaine and jail-overcrowding problem. Its development evolved from a partnership of interests shared by Florida's Seventeenth Judicial Circuit, the BSO, the Broward County Commission on Substance Abuse, the Broward County Commission, the BARC, and the Broward County SAO, to name only the most active participants. Funds were raised locally. There was broad agreement that the criminal justice response to cocaine and crack cocaine offenses for first-time offenders arrested for possession and/or purchase of these drugs should include treatment.

Several of the organizations and agencies involved in this partnership had had prior experience in dealing with drug offenders; hence, they were well suited to tackle the problem. The Seventeenth Judicial Circuit, perhaps more than others, had been dealing with substance abuse offenders, but largely from a criminal justice perspective. BARC, as the county's substance abuse treatment provider, was well versed in substance abuse issues, but less well versed in dealing with criminal substance abuse offenders. Nevertheless, it had been involved in several treatment programs for criminal offenders just prior to the beginning of the drug court. The Broward County SAO had been involved for a number of years with Broward's PTI program. In writing the protocols for who would be eligible for PTI, they formulated the State Attorney's policy position excluding people charged with cocaine or heroin offenses. The newly formed Broward County Commission on Substance Abuse saw the emerging drug court as an opportunity to address this issue and bring together different community groups and individuals to collaborate on a solution.

The successful implementation of Broward's drug court was due to many factors, not the least of which were the personal commitment of the people involved. Judge Mark A. Speiser, Chief Administrative Judge of the Criminal Division of the Seventeenth Judicial Circuit, brought together the different agencies and agency heads in his courtroom to reach agreement on the structure and operation of the drug court. However, Broward's drug court was not born whole and operational. It was put into play and adapted to issues and everyday operational problems as they arose. The local organization and the community base of appropriations and approval out of which the court operates provided the flexibility for this to happen. It did not happen however, without the will of the key players.

Judge Robert Fogan, Broward's first drug court judge, oversaw the day-to-day operations of the early drug court. His efforts and decisions gave it its earliest hue and texture. David Choate, Executive Director of the Broward County Commission on Substance Abuse, in pulling together the different public and private agencies within Broward County dealing with substance abuse issues, kept the drug court on the front burner as a key issue of the commission's strategic plan for dealing with substance abuse. Marie Reynolds, Executive Director of BARC, provided knowledge and resources of BARC and her growing expertise in how best to treat substance abuse criminals. Commissioner John Hart advocated on behalf of the drug court treatment concept with the Broward County Commission and numerous other community groups; he was instrumental in building needed bridges between local government and these community groups and agencies.

There were of course disagreements during the planning and implementation of the drug court. The most central conflict revolved around the issue of whether the drug court should be a postadjudication or a preadjudication diversion court. Ultimately, this conflict pitted Judge Fogan's treatment conception of the drug court, which viewed substance abuse as a disease involving relapses along the road to recovery, against the criminal justice orientation of the SAO, requiring that cocaine users be kept under stricter controls because of their potential threat to the public safety. In the end, this dispute was resolved in the courts in favor of a diversionary model. This was neither a victory for the judiciary nor for the treatment philosophy nor was it a defeat for the SAO. What was decided was that a diversionary drug court is the best vehicle through which the interests of criminal justice regarding the public safety and the treatment needs of substance abuse offenders may be accomplished.

Does the Broward County drug court work? This is perhaps a question that defies an easy answer. Many people have been helped by this program, even though a large number of people who walked through the front doors of the treatment facility during the first year never graduated. Of those who did graduate, fewer of them were rearrested for additional offenses during the 1-year period after they graduated, compared to a group of probation releasees who were eligible for the drug treatment program but declined to participate. In addition, treatment graduates were statistically less likely to be arrested for a felony or for a drug offense than their probationer counterparts. Although program graduates were rearrested slightly sooner than the people released from probation, this difference was statistically insignificant.

Although data are not available for subsequent time periods, this data from the first-year participants of Broward's drug court suggest a positive difference in the recidivism rates and substance abuse levels between program graduates and a comparison group receiving no treatment. Whether the treatment graduates have remained more clean and sober than their probationer comparison group is unknown; however, the differences in their drug rearrests seems to point to such a difference. The definitive answer to this question rests with an examination of drug test data, which is unavailable. The question of whether the difference between first-year graduates and probationer releasees is the result of program effects or the effects of maturation and/or possessing a greater desire to change remains unanswered and awaits further research. Other questions are methodological. They should be raised but not to discredit or detract from the current findings. These questions are raised here in order to help shape a broader context and boundaries with which the findings of the current study may be understood. Until additional research is completed, finding reduced levels of felony crimes, especially crimes involving the use of drugs, suggests that the Broward County drug court has successfully achieved its goal of reducing postgraduation criminal behavior, thus furthering the community's public safety.

Notes

1. FDLE (1989, p. 228) categorizes sales, buying, trafficking, smuggling, delivery, distributing, manufacturing/producing, and cultivating into the single category *sales/manufacture*.

2. Under the authority of the Federal Anti-Drug Abuse Act of 1988, money was provided to individual states for substance abuse prevention. This money came to the Florida Department of Community Affairs, Bureau of Public Safety Management, which in turn distributed it to the counties, in this case, through the Broward County Commission on Substance Abuse. The commission's Substance Abuse Policy Advisory Board reviews grant proposals and selects programs to receive these federal funds in

Broward County. During 1991-1992, it distributed $1,072,00.00 to 15 anti-drug initiatives throughout the community.

3. Diversion may have added benefits. By keeping offenders, especially younger offenders and offenders with no prior criminal records, from associating with known criminals, the chances that the former will develop additional forms of criminal behavior are lessened. Diversion programs are generally less costly than placing people in prison. And diversion programs help manage the size of jail and prison populations.

4. Administrative Order No. III-91-E-1 (June 27, 1991) in the Circuit Court of the Seventeenth Judicial Circuit in and for Broward County, Florida.

5. Administrative Order No. III-92-E-1 (June 27, 1991) in the Circuit Court of the Seventeenth Judicial Circuit in and for Broward County, Florida.

6. Administrative Order No. III-95-E-1 (October 23, 1995) in the Circuit Court of the Seventeenth Judicial Circuit in and for Broward County, Florida.

7. According to Judge Melanie May, a study of the 1995 and 1996 graduates of the drug court was completed July 1997. These findings are discussed in note 15, when felony rearrests are considered.

8. The questions asking drug court participants whether they were living with someone and for how long contain considerable missing data. There were 169 missing cases (21.4%) in response to this question asking them with whom they were living. There were 100 missing cases (12.7%) in response to the question of how long they had been living with the people with whom they were current living.

9. Unfortunately, recent employment information was missing for about 30% of the people entering the Broward County Drug Court during the first year.

10. Last measures on December, 1994.

11. In designing the drug court program, the SAO and the judiciary were in agreement that people entering treatment would be given a 1-year probation sentence; those entering regular probation would receive 2 years of probation. Consequently, a larger proportion of the probation group, compared to those people receiving treatment, were still under state supervision.

12. This is not to downplay the severity of DUI arrests. It is, however, both a traffic and a substance abuse misdemeanor offense different from property misdemeanors such as theft.

13. According to data provided the author in personal correspondence from Judge Melanie May, a study of the 1995 and 1996 graduates of the drug court, completed July, 1997, reported very similar figures. Of the 78 people graduating in 1995, only 10.3% had committed any felony 2 years after graduation. Of the 1996 graduates, only 7% had committed a felony 1 year after graduation. Although these figures are very close to those reported here, their comparison with the current study is difficult because they do not include aliases and offenses committed in other counties.

14. There were 41 treatment graduates and 19 probation releasees rearrested for any offense.

15. There were 22 treatment graduates and 15 probation releasees rearrested for a felony offense.

References

Alcohol and Drug Abuse Services Division. (1991). Untitled and unpublished manuscript. Fort Lauderdale, FL: Broward County Commission.

Broward County Commission Auditor's Office. (1995, March 1). A performance review of the drug court program for the period July 1, 1991 through September 30, 1994, pp. 9-12, Exhibit 6.

The Broward County Commission on Substance Abuse. (1993). *Annual report, 1992-1993.* Fort Lauderdale, FL: Author.

Floyd, S. S. (1997). *Florida statistical abstracts* (31st ed.). Gainesville: University of Florida, Bureau of Economic and Business Research.

Terry, W. C., Rogers, P., & Tomchik, B. (1992). *Alcohol and drug abuse trends in Broward County: First annual DEN report.* Unpublished manuscript.

5. Diverting Drug Offenders to Treatment Courts: The Portland Experience

Steven Belenko

The criminal justice system of Multnomah County (Portland), Oregon has a recent history of developing new ways to process felony drug offenders. Even prior to the establishment of a drug court, key criminal justice and other public officials had embraced drug treatment as an important option for drug-involved offenders and had experimented with various programs aimed at reducing drug use by offenders and incorporating rehabilitation into the court process. For various reasons, however, Multnomah County policy makers remained frustrated that existing treatment interventions did not seem to be effectively addressing the widespread and growing substance abuse problems among offenders. In 1991, they began one of the nation's first treatment diversion drug courts in an effort to reduce drug-related recidivism among offenders and to improve the effectiveness of court-mandated treatment. This chapter describes the context under which Multnomah County's drug court was conceived, the planning and implementation process, the operational process of the court, and the characteristics and outcomes of its clients.

Community Context

Multnomah County, Oregon, is a growing, largely metropolitan area with a 1990 population of 583,887. The county is dominated by the city of Portland, whose population in 1990 was 437,319 (75% of the county population). The estimated population of Portland grew to 497,600 in 1995, a 14% increase. Table 5.1 summarizes the basic population data for Portland (where the vast majority of Multnomah County's felony drug arrests occur).

Portland's population is largely white (85%), with a median age of 34.5. It is a relatively prosperous city, with a median household income of $25,592 and median family income of $32,424 in 1990. The latter was substantially higher than the median U.S. family income in 1990, $23,550. The unemployment rate was 6.2% in 1990, compared with 5.5% for the nation as a whole. Overall, 14.5% of Portland's residents were in poverty in 1989, compared with 11.9% of U.S. residents. However, non-whites and female-headed households in the county were considerably more likely to be in poverty status (Table 5.2): 31.2% of blacks, and 27.7% of female-headed households were in poverty status in 1989.

Public Health Indicators

Several indicators of Multnomah County's substance abuse problems were available from the county's Regional Drug Initiative (1996). Figure 5.1 shows that the number of drug-related deaths in the county has increased substantially, from 38 in 1988 to 91 in 1995. The increase has been greater since the drug court opened in 1991.

The number of births of drug-affected babies has declined substantially, after reaching a peak of 291 births in 1989 (Figure 5.2). Finally, alcohol and substance abuse treatment data (Figure 5.3) show a fairly steady increase in the number of people treated for alcohol or drug problems in the county, from about 12,400 per year between 1986 and 1989 to 17,068 in 1995.

TABLE 5.1 Population and Economic Characteristics for Portland, Oregon, 1990

Population	437,319
1995 population estimate	497,600
Gender	
Male	211,914
Female	225,405
Ethnicity	
White	370,135
African American	33,530
Native American/Eskimo/Aleut	5,399
Asian/Pacific Islander	23,185
Hispanic origin	13,874
Age	
5 years or younger	30,314
6 to 19 years	76,792
20 to 39 years	158,544
40 to 64 years	108,012
65 years or older	63,657
Median age	34.5
Income	
Total number of households	187,262
Median household income	$25,592
Total number of families	104,992
Median family income	$32,424
Total number of males 15 years or older with income	160,193
Median income, males 15 years or older with income	$18,345
Total number of females 15 years or older with income	163,228
Median income, females 15 years or older with income	$11,129
Occupation	
Employed people 16 years or older	218,750
Manager/professional	63,936
Technical/sales/administrative support	70,073
Service	30,333
Farming/forestry/fishing	2,378
Precision production/craft/repair	20,468
Operator/laborer	31,562
Unemployment rate	6.2%

SOURCE: 1990 Census of Population: General Population Characteristics: Oregon 1992. U.S. Bureau of the Census, U.S. Department of Commerce, Washington, D.C.

As the state's population center, it is not surprising that Multnomah County is the epicenter for HIV and AIDS for Oregon. With only 20% of the state's population, Multnomah County has an estimated 3,700 people who are positive for the HIV virus (6.2% of those at risk), two thirds of the Oregon total. Also, in 1995, there

TABLE 5.2 Poverty Status in 1989 (Portland, Oregon)

	Below Poverty	*Total*[a]	*Percentage of Total*
Family			
Married-couple family	3,833	78,690	4.9
With related children	2,556	34,851	7.3
No related children	1,277	43,839	2.9
Male householder, no wife present	900	6,403	14.1
With related children	664	3,466	19.2
No related children	236	2,937	8.0
Female householder, no husband present	5,503	19,899	27.7
With related children	4,893	12,983	37.7
No related children	610	6,916	8.8
Gender			
Male	27,905	206,994	13.5
Female	34,153	220,017	15.5
Race			
White	43,982	362,459	12.1
Black	10,076	32,294	31.2
Native American/Eskimo/Aleut	1,808	5,664	31.9
Asian/Pacific Islander	5,017	22,329	22.5
Other	1,175	4,265	27.5
Age			
Under 5 years	6,204	29,609	21.0
5 years	4,248	5,360	20.7
6 to 11 years	5,665	31,783	17.8
12 to 17 years	4,796	26,652	18.0
18 to 64 years	37,261	273,044	13.6
65 to 74 years	3,534	33,616	10.5
75 years and over	3,486	26,947	12.9

SOURCE: 1990 Census of Population and Housing Summary, n.d. Center for Population Research, Portland State University, Portland, Oregon.
a. Total number of families or people in Portland, Oregon, in that category.

were 59 confirmed tuberculosis cases in the county (9.4 per 100,000 population).

Felony Drug Arrests

Felony drug arrest statistics are available for Multnomah County from the Oregon State Police Law Enforcement Data System, the repository for the State's Uniform Crime Reports (UCR) data (Table 5.3). However, apparent underreporting by some law enforcement agencies and errors in categorizing arrest charges as drug

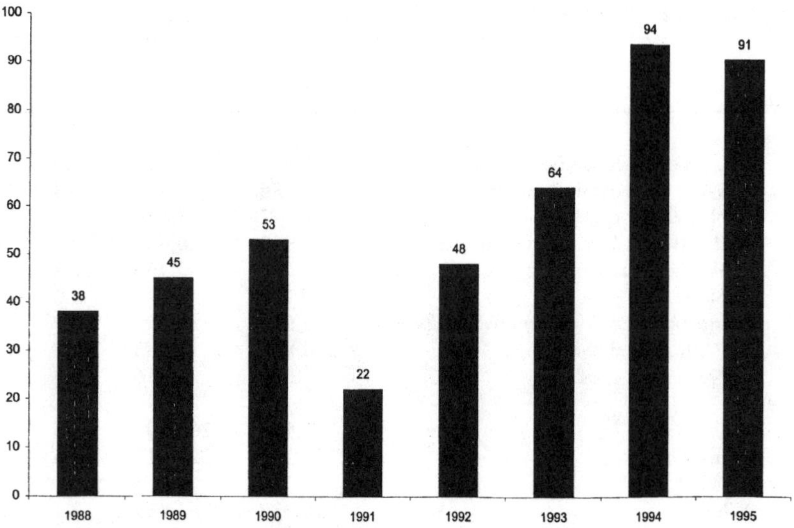

Figure 5.1. Number of Drug-Related Deaths, Multnomah County, Oregon, 1988-1995

SOURCE: State Medical Examiner, Portland, Oregon. Regional Drug Initiative (1996).

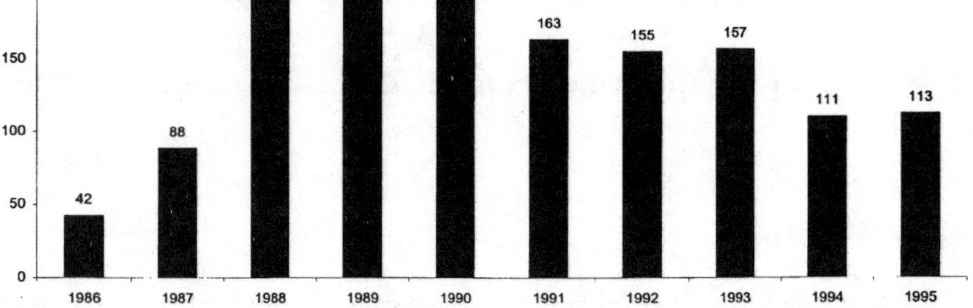

Figure 5.2. Annual Number of Births of Drug-Affected Babies, Multnomah County, Oregon, 1986-1995

SOURCE: The Children's Special Services Division, Portland, Oregon. Regional Drug Initiative (1996).

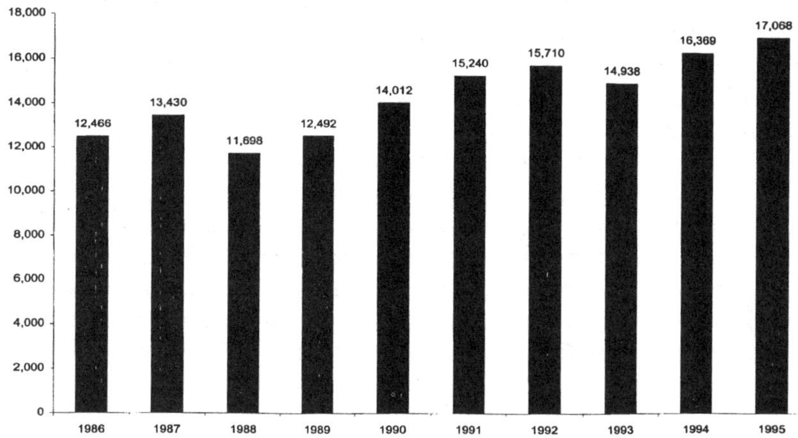

Figure 5.3. Number of People Treated in Public Programs for Alcohol and Other Drug Problems, Multnomah County, Oregon, 1986-1995
SOURCE: Oregon Client Process Monitoring System, Portland, Oregon. Regional Drug Initiative (1996).

TABLE 5.3 Number of Felony Drug Arrests in Multnomah County, Oregon, by Offense, 1989-1995

Number of Arrests, by Type of Drug	*1989*	*1990*	*1991*	*1992*	*1993*	*1994*	*1995*
Opium or cocaine and their derivatives	3,175	2,724	2,927	3,742	3,734	3,141	3,359
Marijuana	963	676	658	611	678	797	1,023
Synthetic narcotics (e.g., Demerol, methadone)	25	16	18	22	77	205	355
Other—dangerous nonnarcotic drugs (e.g., barbituates, benzedrine)	399	281	234	203	294	670	937
Total drug arrests	4,562	3,697	3,837	4,578	4,783	4,813	5,674

SOURCE: Crime in the U.S. (1995). Federal Bureau of Investigation, U.S. Department of Justice, Washington, D.C.

sale or drug possession raise questions about the accuracy of the UCR data. Complete and accurate data on the number of sale/delivery and possession arrests were not available, so all drug arrests have been combined. As the urban population center for Multnomah County, the city of Portland accounts for the bulk of the county's felony drug arrests, so these arrest data primarily reflect trends in that city. Due to the above limitations, the arrest data presented in Table 5.3 should be interpreted with caution.

Although felony drug arrests have remained fairly stable between 1989 (2 years before the drug court opened) and 1994, there was a sharp increase from 4,813 to 5,674 felony drug arrests between 1994 and 1995 (an 18% increase). From 1990, the year before the drug court began, to 1995, felony drug arrests have increased by 53%.

The Court System

The Multnomah County drug court is housed in the Fourth Judicial District of the Oregon Circuit Court, which covers the entire county. The Circuit Court handles all felony criminal matters. Misdemeanor cases are adjudicated through the District Court of the Fourth Judicial District. As of 1996, there were 22 Circuit Court judges for the county; in addition, some of the 14 District Court judges also function as acting Circuit Court judges because of the large felony caseloads in Circuit Court. Circuit Court judges are elected for 6-year terms.

Both the Circuit and District Courts are administered through the state court administrator's office, through local county staff; a state trial court administrator is assigned to Multnomah County. The presiding judge for the Fourth Judicial District oversees both the Circuit and District Courts, assisted by a chief criminal judge responsible for overseeing all criminal matters in the district.

Court Caseloads

As in many urban jurisdictions through the late 1980s and early 1990s, drug felony caseloads increased sharply in Multnomah County. These increases occurred both before and after the implementation of the drug court, but the rate of growth appears to have eased somewhat recently. Figure 5.4 shows the number of new felony cases initiated in the Multnomah County Circuit Criminal Court from 1990 to 1994, by type of charge.

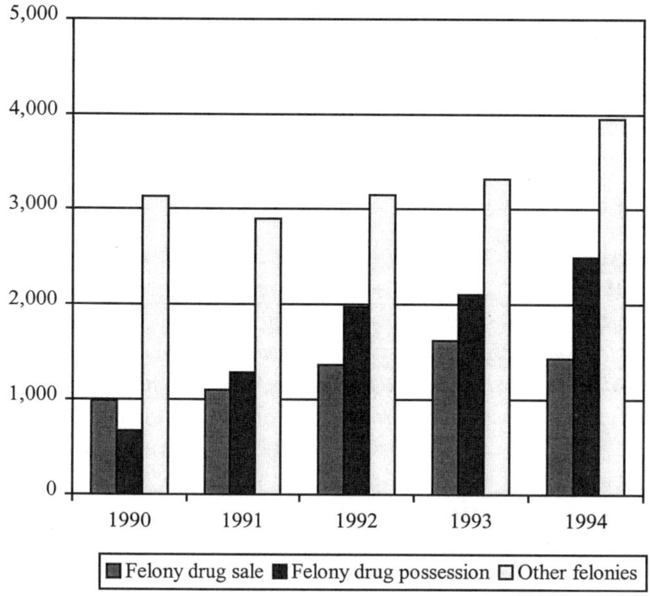

Felony type	1990	1991	1992	1993	1994
Felony drug sale	989	1,100	1,362	1,614	1,428
Felony drug possession	671	1,284	1,974	2,103	2,489
Other felonies	3,132	2,892	3,149	3,319	3,954
Total	**4,792**	**5,276**	**6,485**	**7,036**	**7,871**

Figure 5.4. Felony Cases Initiated in Multnomah County Circuit Criminal Court

SOURCE: Summary of Case Activity for Multnomah County Circuit Criminal Court. Salem, OR: Oregon Judicial Department, 1996.

The dramatic change in Multnomah County's felony caseload is clear from these data. The number of felony drug filings increased from 1,110 in 1990 to 3,917 in 1994, up 136%. Felony drug possession cases, the target population for the drug court, increased even more substantially. The number of new cases increased from only 671 in 1990 to 2,489 in 1994, a nearly threefold jump of 271%. Overall, felony drug possession cases made up 32% of all new felony filings in 1994, compared with 14% in 1990. No data were available on the characteristics of felony drug possession defendants over time, but given the likelihood that the composition of this population did not change much during the 1990 to 1994 period, it is probable that the number of new defendants eligible for the drug court has increased substantially since its inception in 1991.

Felony Drug Case Sentencing

Published data on drug case sentencing in Multnomah County were available only for 1994, so it is not possible to assess how the drug court may have affected sentencing patterns over time. Nor is it possible to determine how sentences imposed on drug court dropouts and failures compare to sentences imposed in similar drug possession cases processed through standard Circuit Court mechanisms. However, given that Oregon has had a structured sentencing system since 1989, it is likely that sentencing patterns have remained relatively stable for drug possession cases. Under the sentencing guidelines, the presumptive sentence for drug possession is probation, with up to 30 days in jail. Observations of the drug court and anecdotal information from the key drug court staff suggest that most program failures are also sentenced to probation for the original drug possession charge.

Sentencing data for 1994 confirm that probation sentences were the norm for felony drug cases in Multnomah County: 76% of the 1,478 offenders sentenced for possession received probation, as did 67% of the 951 people sentenced for drug sale (Figure 5.5). Sentence lengths were higher for drug sale, averaging 34.1 months for probation terms and 13.1 months for prison terms, compared with 18.5 and 4.3 months respectively for drug possession sentences (Figure 5.6). Compared with the state of Oregon as a whole, Multnomah County sentences were more severe for drug cases: During 1994, 86% of the felony possession and 76% of the sale cases in the state received probation sentences.

Planning and Implementation of the Drug Court

The Multnomah County drug court was formally known as the S.T.O.P. (Sanctions, Treatment, Opportunity, Progress) program. It began operation on August 1, 1991, and evolved out of several years of efforts in the county to cope with burgeoning felony drug caseloads, concerns about high recidivism and relapse rates among

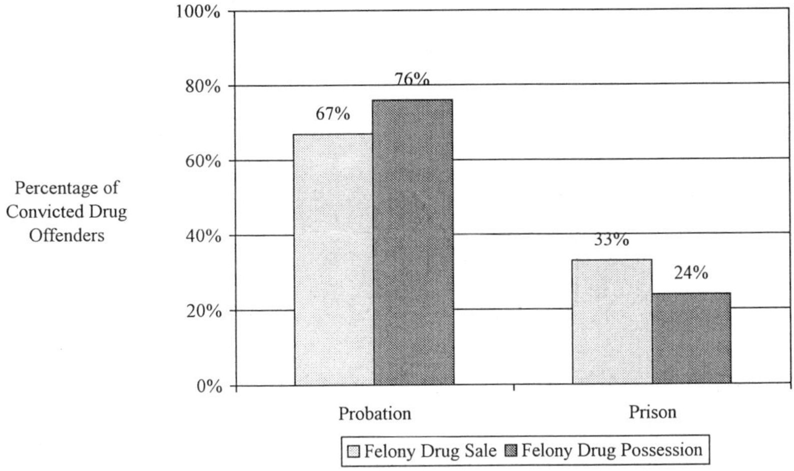

Figure 5.5. Felony Drug Offender Sentence Type, Multnomah County, Oregon, 1994
SOURCE: Felony Sentencing in 1994. Salem, OR: Oregon Criminal Justice Commission, 1996.

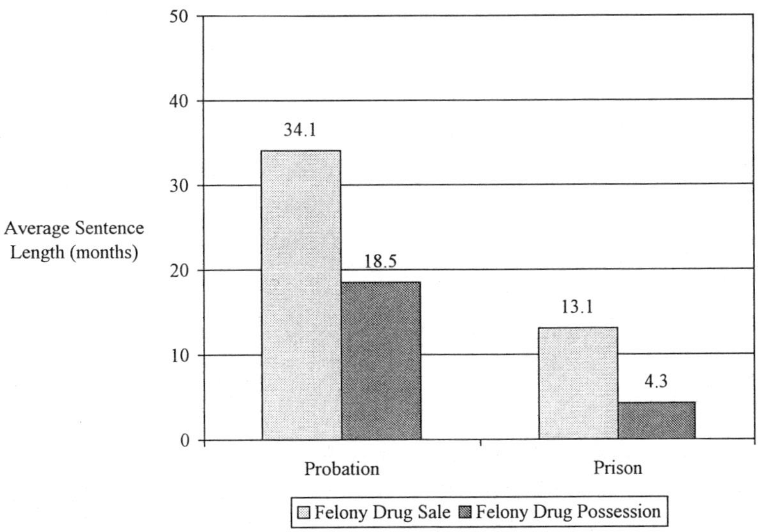

Figure 5.6. Average Sentence Length for Felony Drug Offenders, Multnomah County, Oregon, 1994
SOURCE: Felony Sentencing in 1994. Salem, OR: Oregon Criminal Justice Commission, 1996.

drug-involved offenders, and the typical programmatic and logistic difficulties of integrating substance abuse treatment into the criminal justice process.

The drug court did not emerge out of a vacuum. Prior to its implementation, county court and criminal justice policy makers had developed several initiatives for drug offenders. These included an Intensive Supervision Program for defendants on pretrial release or probation, which included dedicated drug treatment resources; the Drug Testing and Evaluation Program, providing random urine testing and client assessments; and a program called ADAPT that provided a range of substance abuse services to pregnant drug-abusing women. All have been supported by various federal grants. For example, Multnomah County was one of six national sites for a Bureau of Justice Assistance-funded replication of the District of Columbia's pretrial drug-testing and monitoring program. This initiative included urine tests for all new arrestees and urine test monitoring and treatment referral for defendants released to the community during the pretrial period.

Many of these initiatives were planned and developed by a multi-agency task force on drugs and the criminal justice system (Department of Community Corrections, 1993). The Multnomah County Department of Community Corrections, with its Substance Abuse Committee, has also played a key role in identifying drug-related criminal justice issues and organizing efforts to bring key stakeholders together to develop drug treatment interventions (Department of Community Corrections, 1993). The committee has coordinated planning, implementation, management, and evaluation of other substance abuse-related multi-agency projects in the criminal justice system. In addition, the county criminal justice system had previously participated in or conducted research projects in areas such as pretrial drug testing and urinalysis monitoring of offenders. In studying its various drug-offender initiatives, the county has worked with national evaluation groups such as RAND, the Urban Institute, National Development and Research Institutes, and the National Council on Crime and Delinquency. Accordingly, there appears to exist within the local criminal justice community a solid acceptance of the importance of research and evaluation. These research efforts have created a growing body of local knowledge about drug offenders and the difficulties of placing and maintaining offenders in treatment.

Prior to the S.T.O.P. program, formal and informal initiatives were tried to place criminal offenders into treatment. But there were problems in effectively making those linkages. Treatment capacity was limited for criminal justice clients, and there were often considerable delays in getting an offender into treatment. A 4- or 5-month delay was common because treatment was typically not ordered by the court until after disposition of the charges. Moreover, many drug possession offenders were being sentenced to probation, the presumptive sentence under Oregon sentencing guidelines, without any formal judicial order for drug treatment.

The County's Approach Toward Drug Offenders

It is important to understand the context in which the drug court planning and implementation took place. With these previous efforts to put into place new initiatives for drug offenders, and a general acceptance in the Multnomah County criminal justice system of the potential efficacy of drug treatment, there existed the political and philosophical underpinnings with which to create the drug court.

This ongoing concern in Multnomah County about the effects of drug abuse on crime and the criminal justice system, as well as experience in planning and implementing pilot projects to address the problem, created an underlying philosophy that has been articulated by the Department of Community Corrections (1993, p. 13), the agency that has overseen most of these programs. The department's mission with regard to substance abuse is to:

1. Integrate supervision, treatment, and enforcement interventions to ensure that all system components operate in a mutually supportive environment; and
2. Provide timely and effective services for substance abusing offenders, including interventions for target populations with specific needs.

This mission statement is supported by the following points agreed upon by the key drug treatment and criminal justice agencies in Multnomah County:

1. There is a strong relationship between drugs and crime
2. The criminal justice system can improve treatment outcomes and reduce recidivism by mandating drug treatment and establishing linkages with the treatment community
3. Drug abuse is a chronic condition often marked by relapse
4. The effectiveness of treatment can be enhanced by client-treatment matching within a continuum of interventions

5. Acupuncture can be a valuable adjunct to drug treatment (Department of Community Corrections, 1993)

In addition, Community Corrections, which has played such a key role in the development of new criminal justice system initiatives aimed at drug offenders, and which enjoys a close and productive working relationship with the court system, expresses the following guiding principles with respect to substance abuse issues:

1. Chemical dependency is a primary, chronic disease whose development is influenced by genetic, psychosocial, and environmental factors. It effects the physical, mental, emotional, and spiritual well-being of substance abusers and their families. The disease is progressive and can be fatal without effective intervention.
2. Substance abuse is both a catalyst and a causal agent for criminal behavior. Treatment interventions can be effective components of community corrections case management aimed at improving the lives of our clients [and] enhancing public safety.
3. Treatment for substance abuse can be effective. It may require a variety of interventions along a continuum of available services and systematic ongoing recovery support designed to meet individual needs. Interventions include assessment, education, support and self-help groups, acupuncture, outpatient treatment, residential treatment, transitional drug-free housing, drug testing, mental health counseling/treatment, and primary medical care.
4. Successful treatment involves responding to coexisting physical, psychological, economic, social, and family problems.
5. Mandated treatment can be as effective as voluntary treatment. The department will facilitate recovery by providing opportunities for treatment, by working closely with treatment providers, and by enforcing consequences for behavior that is counterproductive to recovery.
6. Successful intervention for community corrections clients requires a high level of communication and cooperation between supervisory and treatment agencies, including joint case planning, joint staffing and training sessions, and other boundary-spanning activities.
7. Early and thorough assessment of substance abuse and related problems is a priority for effective case management and client-treatment matching.
8. Certain populations are more vulnerable and at increased risk for substance abuse problems. These populations may require nontraditional interventions and case management appropriate to gender, race, and culture.

9. Treatment efficiency and effectiveness must be monitored and evaluated through development of measurable objectives, implementation of quality assurance and contract compliance programs, and completion of process and outcome evaluations.

Planning the Drug Court

The S.T.O.P. program actually began as the treatment track for the county's planned Expedited Drug Case Management (EDCM) program. The S.T.O.P. treatment diversion track (the drug court) began operations on August 1, 1991, and the other EDCM tracks began December 1, 1991. The program was funded with a grant from the Bureau of Justice Assistance (American University, n.d.). EDCM programs arose from earlier attempts around the country to use differentiated case management techniques to improve the management of court calendars. The Multnomah County Circuit Court had actually begun a fast-track trial docket in January 1990 to expedite drug case processing. As drug caseloads grew substantially through the late 1980s in many jurisdictions, the Bureau of Justice Assistance began supporting additional special efforts to speed the processing of drug cases, clear calendars so that other felony cases could be processed more expeditiously and effectively, and, where appropriate, link treatment and rehabilitative services to the adjudication of drug offenders processed through special drug case tracks (Cooper, Solomon, Bakke, & Lane, 1991; Jacoby, Ratledge, & Gramckow, 1992).

The Multnomah County EDCM program focused on both drug and property offenders, and in addition to the S.T.O.P. program (the diversion track), it had two adjudication tracks (one for drug cases and one for property offenses) and two treatment tracks to address rehabilitation needs of defendants assigned to the adjudication tracks. The two treatment tracks allowed eligible drug-involved offenders not eligible for S.T.O.P. to be referred to treatment, drug testing, or other services during the pretrial period or following conviction respectively.

Much of the initiative for planning the drug court centered on three key individuals: Circuit Court Judge Harl Haas (the first S.T.O.P. drug court judge), Multnomah County District Attorney Michael Schrunk, and Metropolitan Public Defender James Hennings. As with a number of the first-generation drug courts, the planning process was not as structured as in more recent efforts. The planning process seems to have been largely driven by the close professional relationships among Judge Haas, DA Schrunk, and Public Defender Hennings. Judge Haas had been the Multnomah County District Attorney from 1973 to 1981 and a state legislator prior to that; both Schrunk and Hennings had worked for Judge Haas.

Although they were knowledgeable about the difficulties inherent in effectively linking offenders to drug treatment, Judge Haas and other key officials were initially informed about the treatment drug court concept during a training course on drug case management at the National Judicial College. A visit to the Dade County (Florida) drug court, the nation's first treatment diversion drug court, inspired the planning team to develop a similar program in Portland.

According to the principal drug court planners, the planning process appears to have been greatly facilitated by the good relationships and mutual respect among Judge Haas, the DA, public defender, and Portland police chief. These relationships were also pointed to as important to the program's relatively smooth implementation. However, as in other jurisdictions with diversion drug courts, the public defender was initially somewhat uneasy about the rights that defendants would be required to give up in order to allow long-term treatment diversion: waiving the defendants' rights to grand jury hearing, speedy trial, and filing of search and seizure motions. These waivers were necessary to allow the expedited diversion of felony drug possession cases into long-term treatment.

To build institutional, media, and public support, Judge Haas made a series of community presentations on the new drug court and substance abuse and treatment issues. Good relations with the print and broadcast media also helped to build support for the new program. Finally, Judge Haas and the other drug court planners received strong support from the county court administration and presiding judge, as well as other local government officials.

Drug Court Funding

The original funding for the S.T.O.P. program was a combination of federal, county, and city funds. Federal funding of $400,000 per year was obtained through the Edward Byrne Memorial Law Enforcement block grant program, channeled through the state; it lasted until 1995. Additional funding of $100,000 from Multnomah County and $100,000 from the city of Portland provided the remainder of the annual funding of $600,000 per year. All of the S.T.O.P. program funding supports the treatment services. Grant management for the drug court is provided by the deputy director of the County Department of Community Corrections.

The Bureau of Justice Assistance block grant money ended after 4 years, and current (1996) funding is entirely through county general revenue funds, offset by revenues from client diversion fees and some client health insurance coverage through private coverage or the Oregon Health Plan managed care system. An additional 90 treatment slots for probationers and parolees with nonviolent criminal histories were recently funded through a Drug Court Enhancement Grant from the Drug Courts Program Office of the Department of Justice.

S.T.O.P. clients are required to pay a diversion fee of $400 each.[1] Clients must begin making fee payments 90 days after entering treatment, and clients who do not demonstrate a regular payment record may be sanctioned by the court. The full fee is often not collected until the defendant graduates and obtains employment, although the fee must be paid in full before the charges are dropped following graduation. The collection rate for client diversion fees is less than half the maximum. Between April and September 1996, the drug court collected an average of $8,571 per month from clients for diversion fees. This projects to annual client fee revenues of $102,852; these fees are used to offset treatment program costs. Annual income from client diversion fees thus falls considerably short of the maximum of $240,000 that would be collected if all 600 clients admitted per year paid the full $400 diversion fee.

Guiding Principles of the S.T.O.P. Program

The overall mission of the S.T.O.P. program is to reduce the number of drug-related crimes in Multnomah County by successfully engaging drug users in substance abuse treatment and recovery services. The project's first operations report, covering the first 18 months of the S.T.O.P. program, articulates the following philosophy:

> Our approach is to give the defendant every reasonable chance to make it. Drug addiction is a far more difficult physical and mental health problem than the general public appreciates. Success in a drug treatment program is purely subjective and we need to be more realistic in our expectations. Without a doubt, relapse is a part of recovery and people dealing with addicted defendants need to appreciate that. Any evaluation of drug programs must be undertaken with the understanding that

> most of these defendants are the most needy and difficult clients of our criminal justice system. (Haas, 1993, pp. 13-14)

S.T.O.P. Program Interagency Management

The S.T.O.P. program is operated as a partnership among the Circuit Court of the Fourth Judicial Circuit, the District Attorney, the Metropolitan Public Defender, Department of Community Corrections, and the contracted treatment provider, InAct, Inc. Monthly meetings of the Policy Board, comprising the agency directors and the drug court judge, are held to review policy and discuss operational issues or problems. There are other organizational structures within the Multnomah County criminal justice community that also function in various ways to monitor the drug court's operations. The Fourth Judicial District (Multnomah County) presiding judge, chief criminal court judge, and court administrator hold monthly meetings with the drug court judge and Community Corrections director to review the operations of the drug court and other programs. Furthermore, a Criminal Justice Advisory Committee, comprising key criminal justice officials and the County Commissioner, meets regularly to discuss interagency issues related to the drug court's operations and county substance abuse issues.

Structure and Operations of the Drug Court

The S.T.O.P. program is a deferred prosecution initiative designed to divert drug offenders into treatment. Eligible defendants are those charged with felony possession of a controlled substance, with no significant evidence of drug dealing and with no violent crime charges pending at the time of arrest. Criminal history, whether prior felony or misdemeanor convictions, is generally not considered in determining eligibility for the diversion program.

Program Eligibility

The formal drug court eligibility criteria are currently as follows:

1. Charged with possession of a controlled substance (PCS) I or PCS II and in possession of small amount of drug consistent with personal use;

2. No previous unsuccessful participation in S.T.O.P. drug court and not currently in the program (previous program graduates were recently made eligible at the discretion of the DA);
3. No evidence of drug dealing (based on DA guidelines on amount of drug possessed at arrest);
4. DA not seeking dispositional departure from presumptive sentence of guidelines, and no circumstances indicated to DA's office that defendant will not be able to succeed in the program;
5. No holds or detainers from other jurisdictions and otherwise eligible for "security" release (i.e., personal bond). If current hold, defendant may petition court for acceptance if the hold is later resolved;
6. No other felony or class A person misdemeanors pending or charged in the same instrument, other than traffic offenses or other counts or charges of PCS I or PCS II.

The Drug Court Process

Participation in the drug court is voluntary. New felony drug possession arrests are screened for paper eligibility by the District Attorney's office shortly after arrest. Paper-eligible defendants are offered the program at arraignment, which occurs within 72 hours of the arrest. A day or two after arraignment, interested defendants consult with the public defender and are given an orientation by defense counsel. At this orientation, the defendant is provided with an overview about the drug court and its requirements, along with basic information about the treatment program The first S.T.O.P. court hearing occurs within a few days after arraignment, or 3 to 7 days after the arrest. At this initial hearing, the defendant either accepts or declines drug court participation. If the defendant accepts the program, he or she signs a waiver and agreement form agreeing to (a) waive the rights to a preliminary hearing, grand jury indictment, speedy trial, jury trial, and to call witnesses, to testify, and to contest the police stop and/or search that resulted in the arrest; (b) proceed to a bench trial based solely on the facts stated in the police and laboratory reports if treatment is terminated after 14 days; (c) withdraw from the treatment program within 14 days and return to the trial docket with all rights restored; (d) complete the treatment program to the satisfaction of the court; and (e) not associate with any person using or possessing illegal drugs.

If the defendant accepts the program, he or she goes to the treatment program the same afternoon for an orientation. On entering the program, defendants waive grand jury and speedy jury trial rights, as well as any right to contest the stop and search in their case. They are, however, given an additional 14 days to withdraw, allowing them time to decide if they want to continue in the treatment program and giving the defense time to review all of the discovery materials. However, program data indicate that 80% of eligible defendants are accepted into the program, and very few withdraw during the 14-day grace period.

The program lasts 12 months.[2] Program failure results in a bench trial based solely on the facts as stated in the police report. These brief "stipulated fact" trials are scheduled during the time of the status hearings so that the consequences of program failure can be observed by other program participants. Although during the planning of the S.T.O.P. program, the public defender raised some concerns about the fairness of the stipulated fact trial requirement, it was ultimately agreed to by all parties and appears to have worked well in practice. Under Oregon's sentencing guidelines system, the presumptive sentence for felony drug possession is probation, with an optional short jail term. More severe cases may get a 6-month sentence in state prison. An upward departure from the guidelines is possible where there is a new crime, a long prior record, or other aggravating circumstances. Defendants are sentenced immediately after the bench trial, as part of the monthly status hearings. Clients who fail to complete the program are not eligible for S.T.O.P. upon a subsequent drug possession arrest.

S.T.O.P. program officials have also pointed to this procedure as yielding substantial cost savings compared with the standard plea bargaining or trial process (see below). Whether the stipulated fact trials increase program compliance among other drug court clients has not been empirically tested.

Clients attend monthly status hearings before the judge that also include the public defender, prosecutor, and a treatment representative. At the monthly status hearings, as with most treatment-oriented drug courts, the judge reviews treatment progress, including urinalysis reports, and may make changes in the frequency of testing, type of treatment, or participation in other services. For example, a client with a series of dirty urine tests may be placed in a residential treatment program for a period of time. The imposition of these conditions is based on the recognizance authority of the court. About 50 cases are heard per court day. In addition, nighttime status hearings are held twice a month to accommodate clients with full-time jobs. Present in the courtroom in addition to the judge and his staff are an assistant district attorney, public defender, and a representative of the treatment provider. Any advocacy for the client is generally handled by the public defender rather than the treatment representative. In the Multnomah County drug court, the public defender plays a key role in calling the cases, summarizing the client's treatment status, and responding to questions or concerns expressed by the drug court judge. Both graduations (program completion) and sentences (program failure) are incorporated into the status hearings.

If the defendant has a new arrest charge of drug trafficking, he or she is immediately terminated from the drug program. Clients rearrested on other charges may continue in the program at the discretion of the drug court judge. Other program violations, such as a positive urine test or a failure to appear for a treatment appointment, may simply involve sitting in the courtroom for 1 or 2 days, an enhancement of treatment services (including residential treatment, or repeating a treatment phase), or the imposition of various criminal justice sanctions. The latter may include some time at the Forest Project Work Camp operated by the Department of Community Corrections, a short period of community service, or work release through the County Sheriff's Restitution Center.

Failure to appear in court results in the execution of a bench warrant, and clients who are on bench warrant status for more than 90 days are automatically terminated. If the client has a good excuse for nonappearance, a special warrant is issued pending reappearance. In addition, the treatment provider notifies the drug court if a client does not show up for scheduled appointments. At the status hearings, custody cases are heard first; these offenders are led into court in chains. These are mainly bench warrant cases that had been remanded for short jail stays; they are usually then ordered released and returned to the treatment program. Bench warrants may also result in a short jail term of 2 to 8 days or a placement for 8 weeks in the Forest City Work Camp for offenders who want to return to the program. The drug court is generally fairly lenient in terms of responding to relapses: Termination is only used as a last resort. Data from the program's first 18 months indicated that 28.4% of graduates and 55.2% of S.T.O.P. defendants overall are the subject of a bench warrant at some point during their participation (Haas, 1993).

For defendants who successfully complete the S.T.O.P. program, their criminal indictment is dismissed. Client graduations are held in the courtroom during regular status hearings. The graduates sit in the jury box, and the judge announces their names individually, steps down off the bench, and shakes their hands. All graduates receive diplomas recognizing their achievement. They are also encouraged to speak to the other drug court participants in the courtroom about their experiences in the program. In addition, exit interviews may be conducted with graduates. During the S.T.O.P. program's first 5 years of operation, there have been 950 graduates, an average of about 15 each month.

Description of Participants

Between September 1, 1992, and October 1, 1996, a total of 2,565 drug offenders had been diverted into InAct by the drug court, an average of 52 per month. Of those, 950 (37%) had graduated successfully, 892 (35%) had been terminated, 350 (14%) were currently active in the program, and 373 (15%) had been on bench warrant status for at least 90 days. Among those who graduated or were terminated, the graduation rate was 52%. Including those on bench warrant status, there are roughly 450 clients enrolled in the diversion program at any given time. As of July 1, 1996, the contractual capacity for InAct was 510 (420 for the basic S.T.O.P. program and 90 from the U.S. Department of Justice Drug Court Enhancement grant). This number may fluctuate depending on funding levels.

Recent data on the characteristics of the drug court clients are available from the treatment provider, InAct (Table 5.4A). Almost three fourths (72.6% of the 124 clients who enrolled between July 1 and September 30, 1996, were male, and 67.7% were white. The mean client age at enrollment was 33.8, and 51.6% were unemployed. The most common drugs of dependence were cocaine (including crack; 30.7% of the clients) and amphetamines (28.2%). An additional 23.4% were dependent on opiates (see Table 5.4B).

According to drug court officials, 10% of the clients are HIV positive, and about one quarter have mental health problems, as determined by psychological severity scores during the assessment process.

The Treatment Process

Primary treatment services are provided and managed by InAct, a private community-based treatment provider that operates under a contract with the Multnomah County Department of Community

TABLE 5.4A InAct, Inc.: Client Characteristics, Active Cases Enrolled 7/1/96 through 9/30/96

	Number of Clients	*Percentage*
Race		
White	84	67.7
African American	24	19.4
Native American	4	3.2
Hispanic	12	9.7
Asian/Pacific Islander	0	0.0
Gender		
Male	90	72.6
Female	34	24.4
Education/Age		
Education level at entry	11.6	N/A
Current average age	33.8	N/A
Employment		
Employed	60	48.4
Unemployed	64	51.6

SOURCE: InAct, Inc., Quarterly Report, July 1, 1996–September 30, 1996. Portland, Oregon.

TABLE 5.4B InAct, Inc.: Client Drug History, Active Cases enrolled 7/1/96 Through 9/20/96

Substance	*Level*	*Number of Client Diagnoses*	*Percentage of Clients Assessed*
Cocaine	Dependence	38	30.7
	Abuse	16	12.9
Opiate	Dependence	29	23.4
	Abuse	11	8.9
Alcohol	Dependence	17	13.7
	Abuse	29	23.4
Amphetamine	Dependence	35	28.2
	Abuse	12	9.7
Cannabis	Dependence	26	21.0
	Abuse	19	15.3

SOURCE: InAct, Inc., Quarterly Report, July 1, 1996–September 30, 1996. Portland, Oregon.

Corrections.[3] By contracting directly with a single treatment program, the drug court is assured that sufficient slots will be available for its participants and that the court will have some leverage in obtaining information about participant progress in treatment. And all treatment occurs in one physical location, making it easier for participants to keep commitments.

InAct program staff includes 11 part-time acupuncturists, 12 full-time counselors, one part-time counselor, 8 administrative staff, a registered nurse, and a naturopathic physician and mental health therapist on contract. The executive director has 14 years of experience in the criminal justice system.

Components of the Treatment Program

1. Clinical Assessment—Initial Treatment Plan

Treatment begins with an initial assessment and orientation. During the 1.5 hour orientation session, the treatment program's philosophy and purpose are described. In addition, the clients are told about basic program phases and policies, and the client's rights and responsibilities are reviewed. A Client Handbook is provided that describes the program's philosophy, rules and policies, program services, and client rights and responsibilities. Clients are then introduced to acupuncture through a Health Services intake appointment.

Client assessments are conducted by an admissions counselor. Within 5 to 10 days after program enrollment, all clients receive an assessment based on the Multnomah County Clinical Assessment-3 (MCA-3), used by all county alcohol and drug treatment providers. The assessment process incorporates several other standardized instruments (e.g., the Folstein Mental Status Exam, and a Risk Rating Scale developed by InAct), as well as summary information on criminal history.

The assessment process yields a Master Problem List that summarizes the specific problems that may affect the client's treatment progress. The client's primary counselor, assigned at program intake, uses the Master Problem List as the basis for developing an individualized treatment plan. The plan is developed in conjunction with the client and, when possible, with relevant criminal justice system staff. The treatment plan also incorporates a relapse prevention plan that is implemented before program graduation. It also seeks to address objectives to solve related problems such as unemployment, educational needs, nicotine addiction, physical and mental health conditions, and relapse potential. Each treatment plan is regularly reviewed by the primary counselor, client, and supervisor, and it is updated as necessary. Attendance at community-based self-help groups is encouraged for the client as well as his or her family during all phases of treatment, but it is not required.

2. Stabilization

Clients who require stabilization due to difficulties with housing, mental or physical health, or other serious problems (such as need for detoxification) are placed in a special stabilization group. In stabilization, the clients attend group sessions three times per week and meet individually with their primary counselor once a week. InAct's resource coordinator and primary counselor assist the clients in accessing community services that will improve the client's readiness for treatment (e.g., child care, food stamps, transportation, literacy, employment). Once the client is stabilized, according to the primary counselor and group facilitator, the client can return to primary substance abuse treatment.

3. Phase I—Engagement

This initial treatment phase contains 10 sessions and includes individual counseling sessions with the primary counselor (a minimum of one or two sessions once every 2 weeks), group sessions twice per week, acupuncture three times per week, and biweekly urine testing. During this and all subsequent phases, acupuncture and other medical services are offered to clients as agreed upon by the client and the primary health care specialist.

The 10 sessions offered in this phase include: self assessment, defense mechanisms, thinking errors, and ways to get the most out of treatment.

Clients move to Phase II by attending 90% of all Phase I treatment services, completing an assessment and an initial treatment plan, completing a recovery plan with the primary counselor, successfully completing at least one part of the module on Thinking Errors. The client, group counselor, and primary counselor must agree that the client has accepted personal responsibility for recovery and the need for help in that process. Clients may repeat Phase I if necessary.

4. Phase II—Addiction and Recovery Training

Phase II, Addiction and Recovery Training, contains 32 sessions. This phase includes monthly individual counseling sessions with the primary counselor, gender-specific group sessions twice per week,[4] and biweekly urinalysis testing.

Examples of group counseling topics are:

Drug and alcohol education
Nicotine and alcohol: legal and lethal
Marijuana
Principles of drug action (stimulants, prescription, over the counter drugs, hallucinogens, and opiates)
Emotions
HIV/AIDS
Natural healing
Family and relationships
Gender issues
Values clarification and moral development
Relapse prevention
Leisure and recreation
Support and support groups
Spirituality

Successful completion of Phase II and transition to the next treatment phase requires 80% attendance at all treatment services (group sessions, urinalysis testing, one to one sessions, acupuncture as applicable); completion of a relapse prevention plan with the primary counselor; and agreement by the client and counselor that the client has sufficient skills and information to support the recovery process.

5. *Phase III—Life Skills Training/Monitoring*

Phase III lasts for the balance of the 1-year program commitment and requires individual counseling sessions with the primary counselor at least once per month, monitoring group sessions once per week, and/or life skills training group sessions as identified and available. Life skills group topics include anger and stress management. Other services are available through referral to community resources. Acupuncture is available as requested, and the client continues with weekly urinalysis testing.

Successful completion of Phase III occurs when the client and counselor agree that the client has completed all identified and available life skills training, has adequately integrated recovery skills into daily life, and has met the requirements of the drug court, probation officer, or any other referring agency. The client must have 6 consecutive weeks of negative urine tests as a condition of graduation.

As needed, some clients may be referred to inpatient treatment programs if they are failing to progress adequately in the outpatient program or have repeated relapses. If a client fails to show up for treatment, this is immediately reported to the judge. No excuses are allowed, and the treatment program defers to the judge for the imposition of any sanction or other response.

InAct counselors maintain attendance sheets and progress reports for each of their clients. The progress reports are sent to the judge prior to the monthly status hearing, to allow time for the drug court judge to review the treatment progress for each client and to discuss any problems with the treatment staff before the actual status hearing. Regular meetings are held among the docket clerk, judge, public defender, and treatment staff to discuss program suspensions. In addition, there are frequent meetings between the executive director of InAct and the drug court judge.

Postimplementation Changes

Several changes in the drug court's operations have occurred since the program was implemented in August 1991. First, the original judge, Harl Haas, stepped down as the drug court judge in January 1994. A second judge, Roosevelt Robinson, assumed the S.T.O.P. court bench and served there until January 1996, when Judge Lewis Lawrence took over. Beginning in January 1997, judges were to be rotated into the S.T.O.P. court every 3 months.

After the first year of operations, problems with the original treatment provider led the drug court to issue a Request for Proposals to provide treatment services to the S.T.O.P. program. The original treatment provider had difficulty providing timely and accurate status information to the court at the monthly status hearings. The treatment program InAct, Inc. was selected to begin providing treatment services as of September 1992 and has been the drug court's provider since that time.

In the second year of operations, the drug court began excluding defendants who were on probation or parole, because of concern that there would be too many eligible clients and that treatment capacity would be overwhelmed. Beginning in the third year of the S.T.O.P. program, additional funds were obtained from the Bureau of Justice Assistance Byrne block grant funds to enable the court to accept probationers and parolees. This was known as S.T.O.P. II and had a capacity of 135 probationers and parolees. More recently, a Department of Justice enhancement grant allowed the court to serve an additional 90 probationers and parolees who had nonviolent criminal histories.

Other program service components were added after implementation of the drug court. These include a literacy program, begun in 1993 under a grant from the U.S. Department of Education, operated through the Department of Community Corrections.

As the court has become more institutionalized, some problems have surfaced. The original drug court judge served for over 2 years and was concerned about burnout at times. The problem of burnout with the public defender and assistant district attorney assigned to the drug court appears to be less of an issue because they rotate out of the court about every 6 months. No special incentives are given to assistant district attorneys for the S.T.O.P. program assignment, and at times, it is a bit difficult to get anyone to accept the assignment. Prosecutors tend to be more interested in trying serious felony cases and see these drug possession cases as less interesting.

The drug court judges have also expressed a desire to have more intermediate sanction slots, such as work camps, available for clients who have repeated relapses or do not follow treatment requirements. Although there are a small number of work camp slots available, most clients having problems in the drug court are either jailed for short stays or admonished in court and sent back to the program.

There also is an ongoing need for better statistical information on clients, including follow-up data after the client leaves the program. Although the treatment provider maintains a client management information system and provides regular reports to the court and the oversight committee, the drug court judge does not have computerized access to treatment or client information. In general, the notion of sharing data among agencies appears to be important to drug court officials. There is a consensus that data on additional program impacts and clients would be helpful, and there is agreement on the importance of evaluation.

Measuring the Drug Court's Impact

Only limited research has been conducted on the impact of the S.T.O.P. program on drug offenders or the Multnomah County criminal justice system, so the long-term impacts of this innovation are not yet known. In June 1994, the Multnomah County Department of Community Corrections released a study of the recidivism of the drug court program graduates. The study compared a sample of 54 clients who successfully completed the program with a sample of 50 clients who were unsuccessfully terminated, and it followed the clients for 12 months after program termination. The samples were selected from among all program terminations between July 1992 and March 1994 (307 successful and 264 unsuccessful terminations); sampling procedures were not specified. The results showed much lower recidivism rates for the successful program terminations. About 15% of successful completers had at least one arrest in the year following graduation, compared to 54% of the unsuccessful terminations. The average number of arrests per person was 0.2 for the program graduates and 1.08 for the unsuccessful terminations. About 9% of the program graduates had a conviction in the year following program completion, with 0.15 convictions per person. In contrast, 50% of the unsuccessful terminations had a least one conviction, averaging 0.66 convictions per person. This study did not control for prior criminal records, so these differences may reflect pre-program differences in criminal behavior between successful and unsuccessful clients.

Two recent evaluations of the S.T.O.P. program include process evaluations, analyses of economic costs and benefits, and comparative outcomes for S.T.O.P. clients and other drug offenders. These evaluations will provide important information about the operation and impact of the drug court.

The S.T.O.P. program has several potential advantages over traditional processing of drug-using defendants. First, the defendant enters treatment within 3 days of arrest, as opposed to the 4 to 6 months typical under other court calendars in Multnomah County. Second, the S.T.O.P. program may yield substantial savings in staff time, effort, and funds, helping to offset treatment costs. Potential savings include (a) a reduction in police overtime, because clients' waiver of a grand jury indictment and a jury trial eliminate the need for police witnesses for those who enter the program; (b) reduced Probation Department costs because S.T.O.P. clients are supervised by the treatment program and by the court itself, rather than by the Probation Department; (c) S.T.O.P. participants receive more intensive treatment, urinalysis, medical services, and acupuncture and have more contact with the court, than offenders experiencing standard case processing; (d) under the S.T.O.P. program, all treatment services occur in one physical location, making it easier for participants to keep their program commitments.

In April 1994, the Multnomah County Department of Community Corrections prepared an analysis of the economic benefits of the

S.T.O.P. program. This report estimated that through April 1994, cumulative indigent defense savings had been $392,616 (based on a saving of $246 per S.T.O.P. client), and cumulative police overtime savings had been $319,200 (based on $200 savings in avoided police witness time per case). Additional economic benefits from reduced probation supervision costs have also been cited by S.T.O.P. officials because charges against successful S.T.O.P. clients are dropped, and they are not sentenced to probation (Haas, 1993).

Conclusion

Several characteristics of the political and programmatic context in the Multnomah County criminal justice system helped to facilitate the planning and implementation of the S.T.O.P. program. For example, the key actors in developing, implementing, and overseeing the drug court generally accepted the disease model of addiction and the importance of drug treatment in reducing drug-related crime. Part of this view was the acknowledgment that offenders with long-standing drug problems were likely to relapse while in treatment and that several relapses are often an important part of the recovery process. This attitude has played out in the drug court with a willingness to give defendants several chances to succeed in the program.

Second, as with many of the first generation drug courts, the strong personality of Judge Haas and his influence among his peers and other criminal justice agencies in Multnomah County helped motivate the key stakeholders to buy into the drug court concept. Throughout the planning and implementation process, the key actors appear to have developed and maintained a consensus on the drug court goals, as well as a high level of interagency cooperation. Good community and press relations cultivated from the beginning of the project helped the S.T.O.P. program achieve a relatively smooth start-up, avoiding the tabloid or negative press coverage that has sometimes plagued other drug courts.

Third, the drug court has an integrated treatment program whose program slots are reserved for its clients. The contracted treatment program is allowed to operate relatively independently from the court, and clinical decisions are made by the provider.

Several points should be emphasized about the Multnomah County criminal justice system that underscore the political and programmatic support for the S.T.O.P. program and other interventions for drug offenders. First, the county has a history of designing, implementing, and evaluating innovative programs and services for drug-involved offenders. The drug court evolved from several prior efforts to link offenders to drug treatment. Second, the Multnomah County Department of Community Corrections has played a key role in spearheading new programs for drug offenders and plays an important and influential role within the county's criminal justice system in promoting alternatives to incarceration sentences, fostering a rehabilitative approach to offenders and linking treatment and other services to the court process.

Third, Oregon's sentencing guidelines system, with its presumptive probation sentences for drug possession, provides an existing structure under which felony drug possession cases are sentenced uniformly. This presumption of probation may also provide a context under which treatment interventions become less politically risky for prosecutors and judges. Fourth, Multnomah County's district attorney has repeatedly demonstrated a willingness to support treatment interventions for drug possession cases and other defendants whose criminality is due to an underlying addiction problem.

Finally, Multnomah County's moderate size and relatively small criminal justice community may help to foster the smooth and cooperative working relationships that have generally characterized the planning and implementation of the S.T.O.P. program. The personal relationships that naturally develop within such a community make it easier to resolve conflicts as they arise and reach consensus on programmatic adjustments and changes.

Notes

1. For clients entering S.T.O.P. after January 1, 1996. Clients paying in full within 30 days of admission are given a $100 reduction. Prior to January 1, 1996, the diversion fee was $300 for all clients.

2. The term of treatment may last up to 18 months under certain circumstances.

3. Additional treatment services may be used depending on need. For example, detoxification services, residential treatment, and specialized treatment services for pregnant women are made available for S.T.O.P. clients at several local licensed providers.

4. All Phase II groups are exclusively male or female and are led by counselors who are the same gender as the clients in the group.

References

American University. (no date). *Operational summary of the expedited drug case management program, Multnomah County (Portland), Oregon.* Washington, DC: Author.

Cooper, C. S., Solomon, M., Bakke, H., & Lane, T. (1991). *BJA pilot Differentiated Case Management (DCM) and Expedited Drug Case Management (EDCM) program: Overview and program summaries* (2 vols.). Washington, DC: Bureau of Justice Assistance.

Department of Community Corrections. (1993). *Multnomah County S.T.O.P. Drug Diversion Program.* Proposal submitted to the Center for Substance Abuse Treatment, Portland, OR: Multnomah County Department of Community Corrections.

Department of Community Corrections. (1994). *S.T.O.P. Drug Diversion Program: Program Impacts.* Portland, OR: Multnomah County Department of Community Corrections.

Haas, H. (1993). *S.T.O.P., an early drug intervention and case management program, August 1991-January 1993.* Portland, OR: Multnomah County Circuit Court.

Jacoby, J. E., Ratledge, E. C., & Gramckow, H. P. (1992). *Expedited drug case management programs: Issues for program development.* Washington, DC: National Institute of Justice.

Regional Drug Initiative. (1996). *Drug impact index* (7th ed.). Portland, OR: Author.

6. Experimenting With the Drug Court Model: Implementation and Change in Maricopa County, Arizona

Elizabeth Piper Deschenes and *Rebecca D. Petersen*

The nationwide drug court movement represents one of the most recent innovations in our criminal justice system aimed at decreasing the number of drug-involved offenders by providing drug treatment and intensive court supervision. The drug

AUTHORS' NOTE: Part of this research was supported by Grant Number 91-DD-CX-K050 awarded to RAND by the National Institute of Justice, U.S. Department of Justice. Points of view or opinions stated in this document are those of the authors and do not necessarily represent the position or policy of RAND or the U.S. Department of Justice. The authors would like to thank the Maricopa County Adult Probation Department for their cooperation with this project. In addition, we would like to acknowledge the Principal Investigator, Peter Greenwood, and the RAND staff who worked on this project: Susan Turner, Kathy Rosenblatt, Stella Bart, Terry Fain, Carole Dulisse, and Carolyn Kono.

court program is one among many intermediate sanctions designed to fill the gap between prison and probation. As evidenced by local, state, and national statistics from the 1980s and 1990s, the War on Drugs has taken its toll on the criminal justice system, resulting in large increases in prison populations as well as burgeoning caseloads for probation and other community correctional programs. The situation is worsened by the high rates of recidivism as measured by new arrests for drug offenses and violations of probation or parole. Nationally, inmates sentenced for drug offenses were largely responsible for a 44% increase in the prison population between 1986 and 1991 (Bureau of Justice Statistics, 1993).

In Arizona, the picture is no different from other states. Even though drug offenders accounted for roughly one quarter of the total inmate admissions in 1990 (24% of males and 34% of females), this number had increased substantially from earlier years. In the annual report, the director of the Department of Corrections (DOC) noted that the shortage of beds for the increasing number of inmates was a major concern.

At the state level, some alternatives to incarceration were implemented to help alleviate the overcrowding problem. In 1988, the DOC started a shock incarceration program. Of 639 inmates admitted to the shock incarceration program in 1990, 48% graduated. In northern Arizona, the Community Corrections Division instituted the Intensive Substance Abuse Program in 1988 as a means of dealing with offenders who would otherwise be revoked to prison. However, this program, which involved intensive supervision and monitoring, was very small. Only 62 offenders were referred in 1989-1990, and the success rate was low—37%. In the 1990 annual report, the director of the DOC noted that these "front-end alternatives to incarceration, namely Shock Incarceration, Intensive Probation Supervision (IPS), and the Community Punishment Program (CPP) have not had a significant impact on prison population growth during recent months" (Arizona Department of Corrections, 1990, p. 3).

Locally, Maricopa County, like other jurisdictions nationwide, was also burdened by the high number of offenders with drug problems. Systemwide in 1990, the Adult Probation Department supervised about 23,032 clients. The overall increase in clients from 1985 to 1990 was over 8,500, or a rate of 60%. In 1990, the largest number of probationers, 5,298 or roughly 30% had been convicted of drug sales or possession offenses. The problem has not changed much over the years. As of 1995, the office supervised about 30,638 clients; with 9,628 offenders convicted of drug sales or possession or one third of all probationers.

In addition to the practical problems of overcrowding, judges and prosecutors were not satisfied with the options available for drug offenders (Milkman, Beaudin, Tarmann, & Landson, 1992). Many jurisdictions tried various alternatives such as intensive supervision, but this was no more effective than standard probation (Turner, Petersilia, & Deschenes, 1992). The most recent innovation for drug offenders is drug court. The majority of drug courts currently in operation follow the dedicated drug treatment model. The major goals of this type of court are to link defendants to community-based drug treatment and address defendant needs for more intensive case management and supervision (Belenko & Dumanovsky, 1993). Most of these courts are diversionary pretrial programs modeled after the Dade County drug court in Miami. However, the Maricopa County, Arizona, drug court program is a unique innovation of the drug court model because it was designed as a postadjudication program for offenders sentenced to probation for a first felony drug offense.

The Maricopa County drug court is one of the few postadjudication drug court programs, and it is one of the first programs to be evaluated with a classic experimental design. In this chapter, we discuss the design and implementation of the First-Time Drug Offender (FTDO) program within the social and political context of Maricopa County. Second, we describe the research design used to study the program implementation and impact. Third, we present the results of RAND's 12-month evaluation.[1] Finally, we discuss the major changes that have been made to the drug court program since its inception.

Social and Political Context: Community Demographics

The major metropolitan area of Maricopa County, which is located in the middle of the state of Arizona, is the city of Phoenix. The surrounding towns and cities include areas of varying socioeconomic status, such as Glendale, Mesa, and Scottsdale. According to the U.S. Bureau of the Census, in 1990, the Phoenix area ranked 20th in the United States in population, with a total of 2,122,101 people. The population of Maricopa County was made up of 76.7% white,

16.3% Hispanic, 3.5% African American, 1.8% Native American, and 1.7% Asian (U.S. Department of Commerce, 1992). About 61% of the population was between the ages of 18 and 64, whereas 26% was under the age of 18 and 12% was age 65 or older. In the 808,000 households, the average persons per household was 2.59. Out of an estimated 547,000 families, roughly 13% were one-parent homes.

Because the state of Arizona borders on Mexico, some of the major social problems are related to both the drug trafficking trade and illegal immigrants; yet, there is a significant crime and drug use problem. A total of 3,665,228 offenses were reported to police in 1990, with a violent crime rate of 652.4 and a property crime rate of 7,236.4 per 100,000 (Bureau of Justice Statistics, 1991). In 1989, the arrest rate in the Phoenix metropolitan area was 530 per 100,000 for drug offenses, an increase of 68% over 1980. The arrest rate was higher for drug possession than for sales (339 and 192 per 100,000 respectively). Of all arrestees in Phoenix in 1990, 54% of males and 58% of females tested positive for drugs. Statewide, over 9,500 individuals were clients in a drug or alcohol treatment program as of September 30, 1989. In 1990, the one-day prison population was 14,261 people for a state or federal prison, which represented a 26% increase over 1989.

The political climate of Arizona is somewhat ambivalent. Generally, the state has almost always been viewed as very conservative. However, there has been a battle between the judiciary and executive branches of government, and different forces are at work trying to win over policy makers. Whereas juvenile justice officials support a get-tough policy, the public voted in favor of the medical use of marijuana. Recently, the get-tough policy in adult corrections has been evidenced in the emergence of chain gangs for females. On the other hand, Proposition 200, passed by public vote in the November 1996 election, indicates a favorable attitude toward providing treatment for rather than getting tough with drug offenders. This legislation states that first- and second-time felony offenders convicted of drug possession are required to participate in drug treatment and should not be incarcerated in prison. It is expected that this change may increase the number of offenders referred to the drug court program.

Within Maricopa County, the political and judicial climate are favorable to trying innovative and new programs. As in many other jurisdictions nationwide, criminal justice system personnel in Maricopa County, Arizona, developed various alternative strategies to deal with the problem of drug-related crime. The judges, county attorneys, public defenders, and probation department have always been open to new programming and are often willing to try something creative that is tailored to individual clients and their programming needs. Evidence is found in the plethora of programs that have been field-tested in Maricopa County, including (a) Do Drugs, Do Time, (b) Focused Offender Disposition, (c) Phoenix Repeat Offender Program, (d) Pretrial Drug Testing, and (e) the First Time Drug Offender program.

Structural Organization of Maricopa County's Criminal Justice System

In Arizona, police officers arrest individuals found in possession of even small amounts of drugs. In addition, special task force operations held at night clubs, rock concerts, and recreational areas target illegal drug users from all walks of life. When drug users are arrested, they are usually booked on a felony charge and spend time in jail. The Maricopa County Attorney's office reviews the cases of those who have been arrested for illegal drug use.

Defendants over the age of 18 who have been arrested for the possession of small amounts of drugs and meet certain requirements, such as no prior felonies, are provided the opportunity to enter a treatment diversion program before charges are filed. For those first-time offenders who select this option and successfully complete their treatment program, the felony charge is dropped.

For those offenders convicted of a felony or misdemeanor drug offense, the most common sanction is a 36-month probation sentence. As indicated earlier, the Maricopa County Adult Probation Department handles a large number of felony drug offenses. There are 18 geographic field services units, each with about 11 officers, spread across three divisions.

The primary guidelines for community corrections adopted by the Community Programs Division of the Adult Probation Department were outlined in a Progressive Punishment Plan. This plan called for developing a sentencing matrix that provides increasing control and treatment for drug offenders. The typical response of sentencing judges in the county was to place the offender on probation and to require the individual to obtain treatment. For first-time and/or nonserious offenders, some outpatient programs were offered, but the defendant had to pay for the treatment. When the offender relapsed, often within a short amount of time, the judge usually decided to revoke probation and sentence the offender to prison. The solution was to recognize the relapsing nature of the chemical dependency problem of these offenders and to recommend progressive sanctioning, which would include a treatment component in jail. Unfortunately, neither the Progressive Punishment Plan nor the in-jail treatment component were implemented within community corrections.

Thus, at the time RAND contacted the Maricopa County Adult Probation Department to discuss the drug court program, the county offered either the pretrial diversionary Do Drugs, Do Time program for first-time offenders[2] or more intensive supervision for offenders with serious drug offenses and a long drug history.[3] The major problems with the Do Drugs, Do Time program were that it was not within the probation department, and it was solely a preadjudication program. The only postadjudicative program for drug offenders was the Community Punishment Program (CPP), which involves group counseling sessions three times per week while offenders are on probation. However, CPP was a program for more serious or repeat drug offenders who might have violated their probation or had a previous weapons offense.[4] The probation department did not have any postadjudication programs for first-time drug offenders. As this population made up most of the drug caseloads, the department thought that offering alternatives for first-time drug offenders would be helpful and effective.

Program Design and Implementation

Key staff in Maricopa County's criminal justice system identified similar problems with the handling of drug cases. Their concerns were not identical, but the major problems noted by the court, corrections, and treatment agencies were: (a) the lack of funding for urine testing, (b) the unavailability of adequate treatment, and (c) the overuse of revocation as a response to positive drug tests. Each of these issues played a prominent role in the design and implementation of the Maricopa County FTDO drug court program.

In Maricopa County, the primary problem was the lack of treatment for offenders on probation. The department wanted a postadjudication program to target a large number of clients who posed a minimal risk to the community. If they could intervene through some type of treatment program, the probationers would get off of probation earlier, thus, freeing the probation officers to spend time on their other cases, while simultaneously, the probationers would be involved in drug treatment, drug education, counseling, and other services. The drug court fit along the continuum of treatment and punishment with a population that was not offered anything previously.

For the Maricopa County Adult Probation Department (MCAP), the primary concern was developing a system of supervision and sanctions that would be most effective in reducing drug use and recidivism among first-time felony offenders. Some of the questions being asked by MCAP were whether drug testing was an effective tool for deterring and detecting drug use, and what frequency of testing was most cost effective.

Another problem identified by MCAP was the type of sanctions currently being used in response to positive drug tests (UAs). Officers reported that the most common patterns of responses were to increase testing, transfer the individuals to probation officers with specialized drug caseloads, or refer the individual to the MCAP counseling program (CPP) before considering revocation. Typically, probation officers filed reports of the positive urine tests, and the judge made the decision regarding the action to be taken in the case.

Other primary issues identified by the probation department were the lack of residential treatment and the inadequacy of outpatient treatment services for probationers. Staff in the probation department stated they were more concerned with the adequacy of existing treatment services. Although several outpatient programs existed, probation officers were not sure about the kinds of treatment their clients actually received from them. Furthermore, the programs provided officers with little information on their clients' progress.

The major concerns voiced by the public defender's office were accessibility to treatment and sanctions for positive UAs. They felt that the criminal justice system offered very little for their clients. Those on standard probation were not likely to get intensive treatment and, even if they were referred to treatment, there was little communication between treatment providers and probation officers about cases in treatment. According to the public defender, the most frequent response to positive UAs for those on standard probation was a petition to revoke.

Increasing the use of drug testing to monitor drug use, getting probationers into treatment, and reducing recidivism were the main concerns voiced by the county attorney's office. Because individuals on standard probation were not being tested frequently, they could continue to use drugs without detection, and there was little accountability for behavior.

Designing the FTDO Program

MCAP staff, including two Superior Court judges, representatives from the county attorney's office and the public defender's office, and the lead probation officer, examined both the Oakland, California (Alameda County) FIRST program and the Miami, Florida (Dade County) drug court. The Maricopa county attorney's office and public defenders were very interested in the drug court program. They liked the idea of the treatment levels, drug testing, and the counseling to be provided by Mountain Valley. The public defenders liked the Oakland program, but were concerned about how it would turn out as a postadjudication program. The lead probation officer, Manny Gomez, the primary figure responsible for the design and implementation of the FTDO drug court program, was very much interested in programming for probationers, especially for drug offenders, as there was no program that targeted first-time drug offenders postadjudication. When the program started in March 1992, Judge Susan Bolton was transferred from civil to criminal court to become the drug court judge.

The FTDO Drug Court

The FTDO drug court program was modeled after the Oakland FIRST program, but it was designed as a postadjudication program that could last a minimum of 6 months and a maximum of 12 months in lieu of a 36-month probation sentence. The major components of the program included an initial orientation session and referral to a drug treatment program, followed by scheduled status-report court hearings. During the court sessions, offenders were given a contract that explained the nature of their participation in the treatment program and the system of rewards and punishments. For each class, process group, or 12-step meeting attended, clients received 1 point. For each negative urine test, clients received another point. Based on the point total, clients could receive rewards, including a reduction in the probation sentence and deferred jail time,[5] they could progress to the next phase, or they could repeat the phase or receive sanctions, such as jail time. During each court session, clients were given the date of their next court appearance, which was usually about 2 months from the orientation date. Prior to the status hearing, the drug court team would meet to discuss the treatment provider's progress report and to review recommendations.

The drug court sessions are often used to demonstrate the rewards and consequences of program participation to offenders who are just entering the program. Often, the judge will first call cases who are graduating and then will take cases who are failing. The judge either rewards the behavior with reduced time on probation or reduced jail time and progresses the client to the next phase, or she may require the client to repeat the phase and shorten the time to the next appearance or order more drug testing or jail time. A bench warrant for an arrest is usually filed if probationers do not show up for their court date.

Biopsychosocial Treatment

The enhanced treatment program designed by Mountain Valley Counseling[6] for the FTDO program combined more traditional drug education, counseling, and 12-step techniques with social skills training, relapse prevention, and group therapy. The objective was to treat the whole person and not to simply focus on the drug use, which is regarded as a symptom of other problems. The program had four components: (a) drug education classes, (b) process groups, (c) case management, and (d) aftercare. All probationers assigned to the treatment program underwent an initial assessment prior to entering the program. Individual counseling for the probationer was also available.

The treatment program had three phases. Each phase lasted 2 months and could be repeated at any time during the client's participation in the FTDO program. The initial phase, known as orientation, focused on drug education and social skills training. The client was expected to attend one class, one process group, and at least one 12-step meeting per week, to contact his or her probation officer once per week, and to submit to random urine tests. The curriculum included drug education and awareness and treatment modalities—the 12-step method, the psychopharmacology of addiction, relapse prevention, AIDS and sexually transmitted disease, family roles, codependency, conflict resolution, social skills training (e.g., decision making, communicating, coping with anxiety, developing empathy, dealing with authority, coping with anger), the developmental model of recovery, spirituality, self-esteem, and goal setting. The focus of the second phase, known as stabilization, was on relapse prevention. The client was expected to continue to attend one process group and 12-step meeting per week and to continue to comply with other terms of probation including random urine testing. During the final or transition phase, the client continued attending 12-step meetings and one process group meeting per week. When clients completed all three phases of the program within 6 to 12 months, their probation could be terminated; if they had probation condition, such as community service hours or financial obligations, to complete, they were transferred to standard probation.

Case management was an integral part of the treatment program. The counselor developed individual treatment plans with clients and monitored their progress toward treatment goals. Program phases or classes could be repeated as often as necessary, and clients could remain for a longer period of time in the intensive process groups. They were also referred to inpatient residential treatment and discharged from the treatment program as necessary. The counselor also evaluated the clients' progress and determined whether they were ready to graduate to aftercare.

After completing the three phases of the treatment program, the client could receive aftercare for up to 9 months. During this phase, clients continued to attend a weekly process group. Booster sessions in drug education, the developmental model of recovery, or relapse prevention were offered for clients who were experiencing difficulty in becoming or remaining drug free.

The Target Population

MCAP wanted to focus the drug court population within the continuum of available sanctions. Based on the belief that offenders with different types of drug problems would require different types of treatment and sanctions, MCAP decided to limit the target population for the experimental program to first-time felony drug offenders and to exclude defendants convicted of drug sales or transportation. Thus, the FTDO program was limited to felons sentenced to probation for a first conviction for possession of marijuana, dangerous drugs (cocaine), narcotics, or drug paraphernalia.[7] Those offenders sentenced to special programs within probation, such as intensive supervision or the Community Punishment Program, were excluded.

Evaluation of the FTDO Drug Court Program

RAND's evaluation of the Maricopa County FTDO program was part of a larger experimental evaluation of drug testing and treatment funded by the National Institute of Justice. The main objectives were:

1. To determine whether the frequency of drug testing had an impact on offender reintegration and criminal behavior, and
2. To evaluate the effect of different types of treatment and sanctions on offender reintegration and system overcrowding.

To meet these objectives, it was determined that the experiment would compare four different probation tracks. The first three tracks would vary the intensity of the drug testing schedule and would otherwise be treated as standard probation cases. Offenders on Track 1 had no drug testing, whereas those on Track 2 had random monthly drug testing. Track 3 consisted of high-frequency drug testing, scheduled twice per week. The fourth track, the drug court, varied from the other tracks in terms of the sanctions that were used and the availability of treatment. The classic experimental design entailed random assignment of subjects among the four different conditions.[8] Subjects were followed up for a 12-month period following assignment to probation, with measurement before, during, and after the intervention.

Sampling Plan and Random Assignment Procedure

To construct the sampling frame, cases of all offenders convicted for felony drug possession were screened for eligibility by the lead probation officer at the time of the pre-sentence investigation (PSI).[9] If they met the eligibility criteria for the target population, the probation officer conducting the PSI made a recommendation to place the offender in the FTDO program, along with other recommendations regarding the conditions of supervision. At the time of sentencing, the judge made the final decision regarding the placement of the offender into FTDO. If the offender was sentenced to probation, he or she was told to proceed immediately to the MCAP for further processing.

All individuals identified as eligible for the FTDO program were randomly assigned to the study groups as they appeared for their probation assignment. The clerk at the assignment desk used a computer-generated program designed by RAND[10] to assign the individuals to one of the four tracks and would inform the probationer to report to the assigned probation officer. Probationers in Tracks 1 to 3 were assigned geographically to 1 of 10 probation officers selected to implement the assigned drug-testing tracks.[11] Track 4 probationers were all assigned to the lead probation officer for the drug court program. The random assignment of probationers to the FTDO program began in March 1992, a few months after the beginning of the evaluation, and continued until April 1993.

Data Sources

Each individual was followed up for a period of 12 months following random assignment. Several sources of data were used including the probation files (containing the criminal record history, the pre-sentence investigation report, and the terms of probation), the chronological files maintained by the probation officer, and the LEJIS record system.[12] Baseline information was coded from the probation files including the demographic characteristics of individuals referred to court (race, sex, education, employment, marital status), prior criminal record (juvenile and adult arrests and convictions), prior criminal justice system intervention, substance use history, prior drug treatment, current offense information, and risk/need assessments. Most of this information was obtained from the PSI report. With the exception of the data on prior substance use history and treatment intervention, the data were highly valid and reliable. Because MCAP does not use a screening instrument or objective criteria to measure prior drug use, this information was less reliable.[13] Details on the current offense and sentence and the conditions of probation were found on the Sentencing Report and Terms of Probation Form.

The primary measures of program implementation included the number and type of services received and the nature of the case management for both experimental and control offenders during their follow-up. The number and type of face-to-face and phone contacts with clients, the extent and nature of monitoring checks performed (e.g., criminal record checks, employment verification), and the number of drug and alcohol tests requested by the probation officer were recorded from probation files. Information about referrals to treatment, the duration of treatment, and the types of counseling and education provided, as well as the dates of the court review hearings and the judicial decisions, were coded from the progress reports in the probation files.

RAND's evaluation was designed to measure the impact of probation with and without drug testing and drug court with treatment on a range of outcomes, including drug use, involvement in drug treatment, drug test results, rearrest record, drug-related criminal activity, employment and other socially productive behavior, and justice system costs. Outcome data were gathered from probation files, which include the probation officer's reports of the individual's behavior while on probation, the progress reports from the treatment programs in which the offenders participate, and the results of urinalysis tests and the action taken in response to positive tests. Data on technical violations, new felony arrests, and sanctions were recorded from both the probation officer files and the LEJIS system.[14]

Study Findings

The RAND evaluation included a sample of 630 offenders who were randomly assigned to the four different conditions. A total of 176 probationers were assigned to Track 4 (drug court), and the other 454 were fairly evenly divided among Tracks 1, 2, and 3. In the following sections, we describe the characteristics of these offenders, their participation in drug court, and the major outcome findings comparing the drug court to those on standard probation.[15]

Sample Characteristics

There were no statistically significant differences between those probationers randomly assigned to standard probation and those assigned to drug court. About three quarters of the group were male, and almost 50% were white; about 28% were Hispanic, and 22% were African American; less than 20% were married. Over half did not have a high school diploma, and just less than 50% were unemployed at the time of their current arrest. These first-time felony drug offenders had started using alcohol or drugs at the age of 16 and were frequent drug users or dependent on drugs by the time they were in their early twenties. After alcohol, the primary drug of choice was marijuana for about half of the probationers, and a history of prior cocaine use was indicated for 40%. Less than 20% had a history of methamphetamine use or abuse, and even fewer had used or abused other types of drugs (heroin, PCP, LSD, etc.). Almost 40% had a history of prior substance abuse treatment, and less than 20% reported being drug dealers. The history of substance use and dealing among this sample of felony drug offenders makes them similar to drug offenders on probation in other jurisdictions,[16] with the exception of a lower reporting of crack cocaine use.

The criminal history of this sample appears to be similar to other first- or second-time felony offenders in drug courts nationwide. These probationers have, on average, almost five prior arrests and have been in jail or on probation once before, having first been convicted at age 23. The type of current offense distinguishes this sample from other drug court populations.[17] About 34% were charged with possession of drug paraphernalia, another 30% with possession of marijuana, 26% with possession of narcotic drugs, and 10% with possession of dangerous drugs. The probationers in Maricopa County were sentenced to an average of 35 months probation.

Program Implementation

There were several differences in the design of the drug court program that changed the conditions of probation. For example, drug court participants had fewer in-person contacts and more telephone contacts with the probation officer than those on standard probation and more contacts with other members of the drug court team, including the treatment counselor and judge. Perhaps the most important difference between the drug court program and the probation tracks was the significantly lower level of drug testing for those in drug court than for those on probation. On average, over the 12-month period, those in drug court were tested once every 2 months, whereas those on standard probation were tested once a month.[18]

A major objective of the FTDO program was to increase the number of probationers who participated in drug treatment. Because the treatment program was a mandatory part of drug court participation, the majority of offenders assigned to drug court participated in treatment during the 12-month follow-up, with the exception of those persons who never showed up for court or for treatment. As

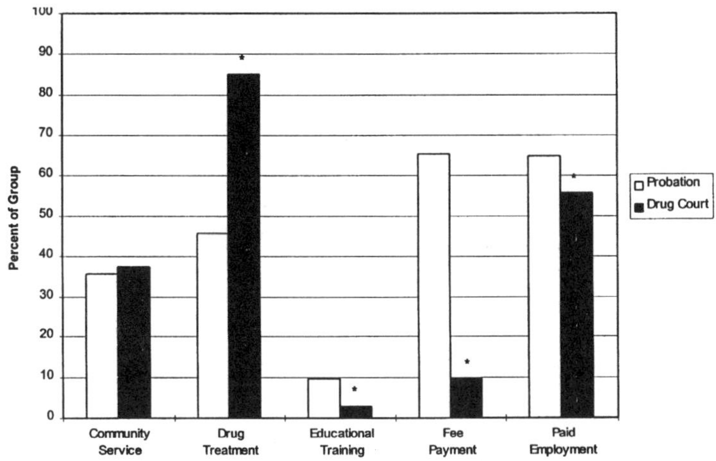

Figure 6.1. Participation in Program
NOTE: Significant difference between groups, $p = .05$.

shown in Figure 6.1, whereas 85% of drug court clients participated in drug education and treatment and attended outpatient counseling, less than half of those on standard probation received any drug treatment. On the other hand, drug court clients were less likely to comply with all of the conditions of their probation sentence. Some of the other differences shown in Figure 6.1 included lower levels of employment and lower rates of fee payment among drug court participants than among those on probation.

Program Outcomes

Prior studies have shown that coercion into treatment increases the retention in treatment (Anglin & Hser, 1990); thus, we expected a reasonably high success rate among those in drug court. Figure 6.2 indicates that 61% of offenders assigned to drug court could be called successes: either completing the treatment program or still in treatment at 12 months. Within this group, a total of 30% successfully graduated and were discharged from probation. Another 11% graduated from the program but were transferred to standard probation to complete the conditions of their sentence, such as community service hours. At the end of the 12-month follow-up, about 18%

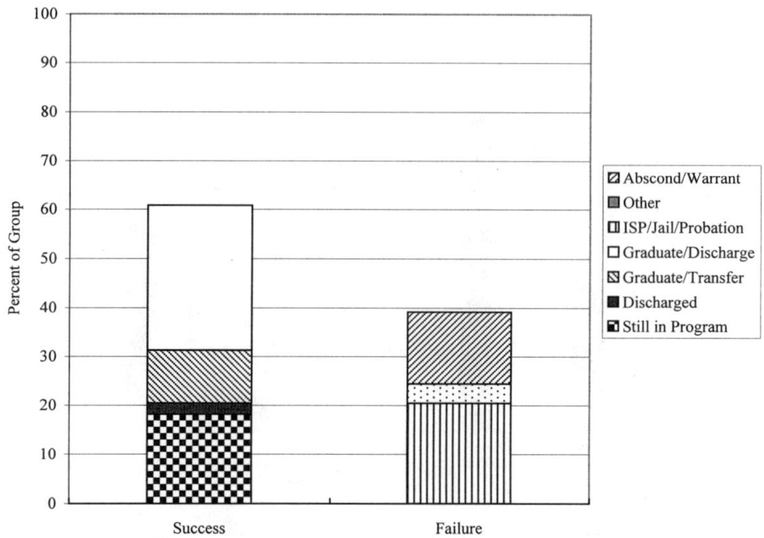

Figure 6.2. Drug Court Program Status at 12 Months

of those assigned to drug court were still in the treatment program because they started late or had to repeat one or more phases of the program. A small proportion (2%) were discharged while still in the program.[19]

Among the 39% with unfavorable outcomes (failure) at the end of the 12-month period, 15% absconded or had a warrant out for their arrest, and 4% were terminated for some other reason. About 21% received a sentence of ISP, jail, or prison for a technical violation or new arrest. Some of these offenders may have returned to the drug court program after serving these sentences to complete the drug treatment program, because a technical violation or new arrest did not necessarily mean that they were terminated.

The differences between drug court and probation resulted in reduced time on probation and therefore lower costs. On average, over the 12-month period, those in drug court spent 256 days on probation, 37 days in jail, 4 days in prison, and 27 days free, whereas those assigned to probation spent 279 days on probation, 36 days in jail, and 13 days in prison. The average cost for drug court was $2,795 per year per individual, compared to $2,926 for standard probation.

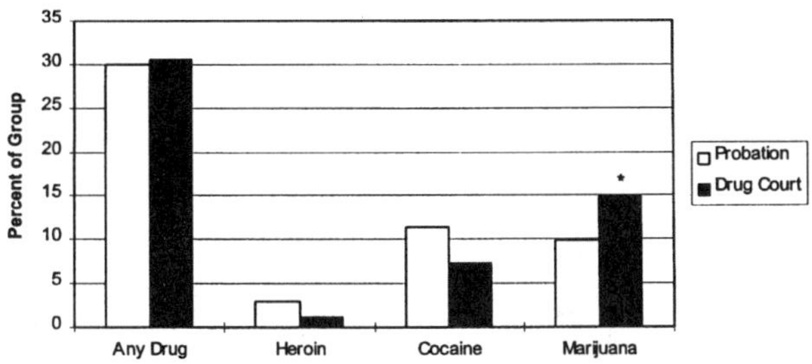

Figure 6.3. Percentage of Positive Drug Tests Within 12 Months (tested offenders only)

NOTE: Significant difference between groups, $p = .05$.

Substance Use

Regardless of differences in program implementation and participation during the 12-month follow-up, there were few differences between those who participated in drug court and those on standard probation in terms of outcomes. The drug court program did not reduce overall substance use, as measured by the proportion of urinalysis tests that were positive. As shown in Figure 6.3, about 30% of tested offenders were positive. As for specific drugs, the only statistically significant difference was a higher proportion of positive tests for marijuana among drug court clients than among standard probationers. This was offset by rates of cocaine and heroin use that were lower among drug court clients, but not significantly so.

Recidivism

One measure of program success or failure is the nature and extent of recidivism among program participants. The results of the RAND experiment indicated that there were no significant differences between offenders on standard probation and those in drug court in the prevalence and frequency of new felony arrests during the 12-month follow-up period. Figure 6.4 indicates that 30% of each group had a new arrest. Nor did the drug court program have an impact when measured as new conviction. On the other hand, looking at the consequences, one sees a difference in terms of how many probationers were sent to prison in comparison to drug court clients (23% versus 9%).

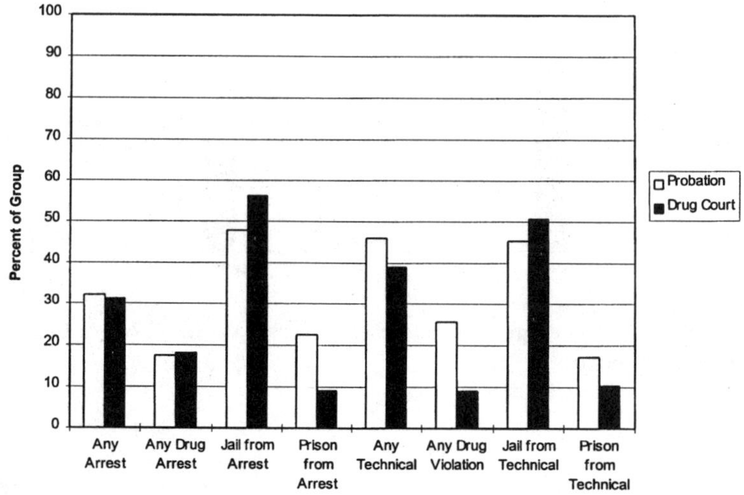

Figure 6.4. New Arrests and Technical Violations in 12 Months
NOTE: Significant difference between groups, $p = .05$.

The drug court program did not appear to have a significant impact on the timing of new arrests. Survival analysis of time to first felony arrest, shown in Figure 6.5, indicated that within the first 90 days (or 3 months), drug court clients had the lowest rate of failure. By 6 months, at least 15% of both groups of individuals referred to the evaluation had a new arrest. Although the difference was not

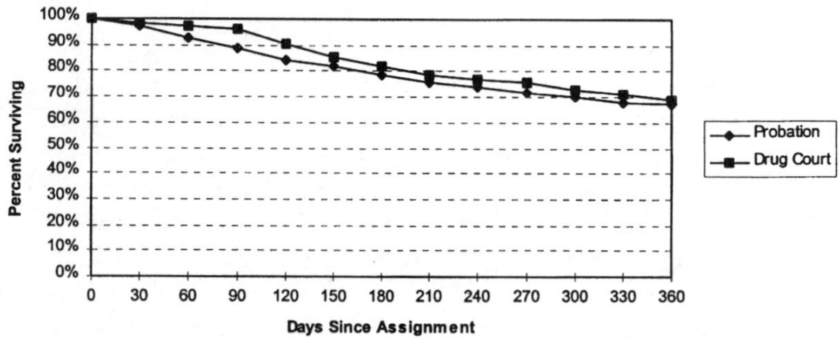

Figure 6.5. Time to First Felony Arrest
NOTE: chi-square = .63, n.s.

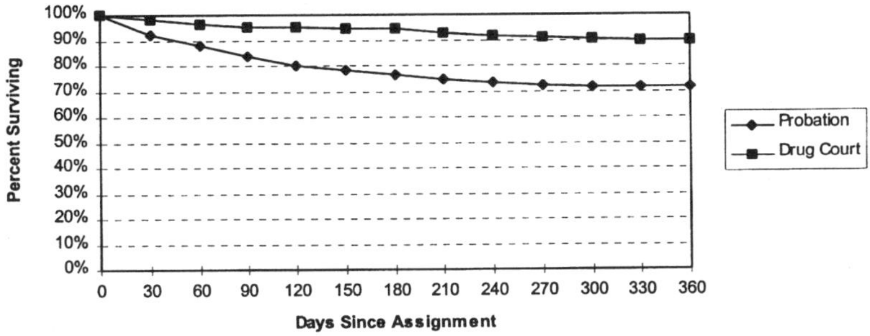

Figure 6.6. Time to First Technical Violation for Drugs
NOTE: chi-square = 22.8, $p < .0001$

significant, drug court participants did seem to fail at a slower rate for all felony arrests.

There were no differences between drug court and probation in the proportion of offenders with a technical violation (about 40% indicated in Figure 6.4). However, significantly fewer drug court clients (9%) in comparison to those on standard probation (26%) had a drug-related technical violation. As shown in Figure 6.6, those on standard probation violated the conditions of their probation more quickly.[20]

Changes to the Drug Court Program

Near the end of the field experiment, MCAP had to decide whether to continue the program and how it would be funded, because the original funding for the FTDO program had been part of the RAND evaluation. Both probation officials and clients appeared to like the program, and initial statistics suggested that the FTDO program increased the number of clients in treatment. Consequently, MCAP decided the drug court should be institutionalized. However, funding was one of the major issues. The estimated costs of continuing the contract with a private agency appeared to be too high. In addition, during the transition period, the number of clients dropped from between 100 and 150 active clients to about 30, and the program almost died. Although the department wanted the program, they were not sure how to increase the number of clients.

Two major changes were initiated in 1994. First, MCAP received approval to hire an in-house chemical dependency counselor and the contract with Mountain Valley Counseling was discontinued. One reason for the change was that it was more cost-effective to hire an in-house counselor. Other reasons were that the department would be able to have better coordinated contact with the counselor, delivery of services, and strategic planning, with the service being provided in-house. An in-house probation officer who had prior experience as a drug counselor was hired early in the fiscal year. The second change was to require the clients to pay a counseling service fee of $16 per session, rather than provide treatment free of charge. These two changes allowed MCAP to continue the drug court program and to have greater control over its design and implementation.

The Maricopa County drug court program has gone through several modifications since these initial changes in 1994, in a continuing effort to enhance and improve the program. MCAP is using a strategic planning teamwork approach that involves support staff, probation officers, drug counselor, county attorneys, defense attorneys, and judges. The major stakeholders taking part in the drug court strategic planning decided to redefine the drug court curriculum to include a more cognitive model of drug treatment, relapse groups, life-skills training, and financial planning. In addition, the new drug court program (see Figure 6.7) includes three phases, with a pretreatment phase designed to get clients ready for drug treatment while awaiting entry into the program.[21] Many of the changes that have been made following the RAND experiment appear to be in direct response to the study findings.

The frequency of drug testing is an important aspect of any drug treatment program. Some drug court programs, such as the one in Los Angeles County, require daily drug testing. The logic behind the high frequency of testing in these programs is to increase the accountability of clients. In LA County, the daily testing appears to work well for drug court clients (Deschenes & Torres, 1996). On the other hand, the results of some studies of probationers have indicated that frequent testing leads to more probation violations (Deschenes, Turner, Greenwood, & Chiesa, 1996; Turner et al., 1992). The FTDO experiment was designed so that drug court clients would be tested an average of once or twice a month, which was the same frequency as people on standard probation. However, in implementing the FTDO drug court program, the drug treatment

Program Phase	*Treatment Schedule*	*Urinalysis Schedule (Random)*
Pretreatment	7.5 hours: 1.5 hours Intake, plus 1.5 hours once per week for 4 weeks	2 tests per month minimum
Path I	20 hours: 2.5 hours once per week for 8 weeks	4 tests per month minimum
Path II	16 hours: 2 hours once per week for 8 weeks	2 tests per month minimum
Path III	16 hours: 2 hours once per week for 8 weeks	2 tests per month minimum

Figure 6.7. The Maricopa County Adult Probation Department's Drug Court Program: Basic Structure of Drug Court Treatment and Urinalysis

NOTE: All program phases include weekly 12-step program participation.

counselor was the one to actually determine the frequency of testing. Whereas the results of the experimental study showed that drug court clients were being tested an average of about once per month, the counselor reported that testing was done on an "as needed" basis. In other words, if the counselor felt the person had been using or thought it was time for the individual to be tested, then a test would be required.

In redesigning the drug court program within the probation department, special consideration has been given to the minimum frequency of drug testing and the type of sanctions to be used. The new program recognizes the likelihood of relapse during the initial pretreatment phase and thus tests clients an average of twice per month. However, once the clients have been moved to Path I, they are tested a minimum of four times per month on a random basis. The drug-testing component is now being provided by the Treatment Assessment Screening Center (TASC), and the testing is randomized using a color-coded system.[22] Based upon the randomization of the color system and the individual's phase level, the probationer could be tested anywhere from twice a month to five times a month. The number of drug-testing sites has also expanded: Three TASC sites in the valley are used for the drug court program, making it much easier for clients. Moving the drug-testing component to TASC has made it less cumbersome (it no longer takes up time that is used in counseling sessions) and makes it more difficult for clients to manipulate the system.

Another significant change in the drug court program was the addition of a special component for offenders with positive drug tests. The results of the RAND experiment indicated the rate of positive drug tests was similar for both drug court clients and those on standard probation. Consequently, the new drug court program has added a relapse prevention component. Those clients who have a positive drug test, or miss or have a diluted UA, are required to attend additional counseling sessions that focus on the problem of relapse and how it can be prevented. Individuals are also required to attend at least five 12-step meetings per week, rather than the usual one per week. Participation in the additional relapse prevention treatment lasts for 4 weeks.

One of the other weaknesses of the FTDO program was the lack of program participation in terms of mandatory probation requirements, such as maintaining employment, job hunting, or payment of probation fees or fines. In addition, roughly 11% of drug court clients were continued on probation following completion of the drug court program because they had not completed their community service hours or paid their fees. By moving the drug court program in-house, the probation officers are able to emphasize the importance of meeting the probation requirements and to work more closely with those individuals needing help.

As noted previously, the original FTDO drug court program was modeled after the Oakland FIRST program. The primary feature of this program that makes it different from other drug courts is the use of a contractual system that specifies consequences and rewards for compliance with the program. In the FTDO program, contracts were usually written on a 2-month basis. Occasionally, 1-month contracts were used if clients were going to repeat a phase or if they needed to maintain closer contact with the judge. As indicated earlier, several modifications have been made to the new drug court program, changing the system of sanctions and rewards to create more flexibility. During the pretreatment phase and Path I, clients are required to appear in court once every 4 weeks, thereby requiring more frequent contact with the judge and closer monitoring by the probation counselor. In addition to the new relapse prevention component, which is a new sanction imposed on offenders with positive drug tests, those offenders who are delinquent in payment of court-ordered fees must attend a financial group. The financial group provides assistance with job skills and money management.

The major difference between the original FTDO program and the new drug court is an increased emphasis on cognitive behavioral modeling and relapse prevention. The new drug court includes program modules taught by the probation officers and treatment counselors that are designed to increase individual's behavioral changes, such as life-skills training and financial counseling. Because prior research has indicated that successful correctional programs include cognitive behavioral techniques (Andrews et al., 1990), it is hoped that the new drug court program will have higher program completion and success rates.

Conclusion and Policy Implications

Careful consideration was given to the design and implementation of the drug treatment program in Maricopa County, Arizona. The primary stakeholders interested in the program were members of MCAP's Programs Division. MCAP targeted first-time felony offenders sentenced to probation for drug court because they represented a large segment of those on probation and there were no existing postadjudication treatment programs for this group. In addition, the drug court program offered an alternative that fit within the continuum of treatment and sanctions offered by MCAP. Overall, the drug court component was attractive to MCAP staff because it would provide different types of counseling and education for which the defendant didn't have to pay. One of the other goals of the drug court program was to reduce time on probation and time in jail. The drug court would offer this opportunity if offenders successfully completed the drug court program requirements and the probationers could be successfully terminated from the program in 6 months and the 60-day deferred jail sentence dropped. If offenders successfully completed drug court but still owed money or had community service hours, the Programs Division decided to place them on standard probation until they paid their fines and/or completed all of their community service hours.

The results of RAND's first evaluation of the FTDO drug court program indicate the program was fairly well implemented in terms of the levels of participation in drug education classes, counseling, and treatment. However, some clients referred to the drug court never appeared for drug treatment with the private provider; thus, only 85% received the program as designed. Nonetheless, 61% of all those assigned to drug court either graduated or were still in the program at the 12-month follow-up date. Even though some individuals did not participate in the drug court program, there were some statistically significant differences between offenders assigned to the drug court program and those on standard probation.

The results of RAND's 12-month follow-up evaluation show the Maricopa County drug court is having a significant impact on the proportion of probationers who are referred to, participate in, and successfully complete a treatment program. It also appears to have significantly reduced the time participants spend in prison. Otherwise, the difference in treatment participation levels does not appear to have translated into meaningful reductions in drug use or recidivism during the 12-month program.

Initial results of a 3-year follow-up of 506 out of the 630 original sample are more encouraging (Turner, 1997). One third of offenders assigned to drug court had a new arrest compared to 44% of offenders on probation. Drug court participants also had significantly lower rates of technical violations than those on standard probation (64% versus 75%). Thus, it appears in the long run that the drug court program has significantly reduced recidivism.

Since the completion of the field experiment, the drug court treatment component was moved within probation, and the program has expanded considerably. As of October 1997, there were over 180 offenders in drug court, with a staff of three probation officers, two chemical dependency counselors, and a drug court judge. Enhancements to the drug court program, including a pretreatment phase, increased and randomized drug testing, and relapse prevention and financial counseling groups, have increased the program completion rate to 71%. The refined drug court program now offered by MCAP is an example of a well-structured program that provides needed services and treatment for drug offenders.

Proponents of the Maricopa County, Arizona, drug court program are encouraged by the increased number of individuals who have successfully participated in and graduated from drug court since several modifications were made in 1994. The decision to implement a postadjudication drug court appears to have been a wise policy decision. With continued strategic planning by the drug court team, this unique innovation should continue to provide important treatment and services for drug offenders and may help to reduce substance use, recidivism, and prison overcrowding.

Notes

1. The evaluation continued for another 36 months with funding from the National Institute on Drug Abuse. A report is currently being prepared by Susan Turner and Peter Greenwood.

2. The Do Drugs, Do Time program encompasses law enforcement, prosecution, treatment, education, and the media. The treatment program is conducted by TASC, Treatment Assessment Screening Center, a nonprofit corporation in Phoenix, in conjunction with the County Attorney's office. The length and fees of the program vary depending on the individual's need. All fees are waived if the defendant is indigent, and a sliding scale is available and based on the person's ability to pay. TASC provides a variety of services to the county and state including urinalysis and breath-alyzer testing, educational programs, client assessment, counseling, and substance abuse treatment.

3. Both the Community Punishment Program and Intensive Probation Supervision involve more frequent contacts between probationers and officers; neither required more frequent drug testing, nor were they specifically designed for drug offenders. On the other hand, those clients who were targeted for CPP or IPS at pretrial were not eligible for the drug court program. Probationers sentenced to CPP or IPS often had prior felony arrests. Neither of these programs changed after the drug court program was initiated.

4. CPP is a special term of probation for those offenders who are determined to be prison bound during the pre-sentence investigation.

5. Most of the convicted offenders receive a 36-month term of probation and 60 days of deferred jail.

6. Mountain Valley Counseling was selected by RAND staff to be the treatment provider for the FTDO program based on a competitive bid.

7. Eligible participants could have prior felony convictions for nondrug offenses.

8. Randomized designs provide the most direct way of assessing the impact of an intervention and help assure the validity of the study findings (Dennis, 1988).

9. A positive answer to any of the following four questions excluded the defendant from eligibility for the drug court program: (a) Is there a need for inpatient counseling? (b) Does the case require CPP counseling? (c) Is there a need for specialized caseload supervision? and (d) Is the defendant appropriate for FARE probation?

10. The computer program specified predetermined proportions for each track (initially one quarter to each track, then one half to Track 4 to fill the available slots, with one third of the other offenders to each of the three remaining tracks), and assignments were given as each name was entered into the computer.

11. The probation officers with FTDO clients carried a normal caseload, and the additional FTDO clients did not increase the caseload; they represented probationers who would have been assigned to these officers, regardless of the experimental drug-testing conditions.

12. The LEJIS system is the computerized tracking system maintained by the probation department to record the current status of an offender and his or her prior record.

13. The lack of adequate data on substance use histories is common to most agency files within the criminal justice system. More reliable and accurate information is usually found in a treatment provider's files. Because only one fourth of our sample

would definitely be in treatment, we had to collect the best information possible from the larger source, for example, the probation files.

14. Arrests for violations of probation were counted as technical violations not as new arrests.

15. These analyses group together the three drug testing tracks. For a complete report, see Deschenes et al. (1996).

16. See, for example, Turner et al. (1994).

17. See, for example, Goldkamp and Weiland (1993).

18. This is the average of tests taken (not tests ordered) for those assigned to no testing, random once a month testing, and frequent (twice per week) testing. When compared to those on random testing, there was no difference between drug court clients and probation in the mean number of tests taken.

19. These individuals either had shorter terms of probation or were discharged due to medical conditions or age.

20. Part of the reason is that those who were tested more frequently were more likely to have a positive drug test.

21. The pretreatment phase was initiated when there were too many clients waiting to enter drug court and not enough program slots due to the existence of a single chemical dependency counselor.

22. Clients are given a certain color and call TASC every day. If theirs is the color of the day, they go in for a UA.

References

Andrews, D. A., Zinger, I., Hoge, R. D., Bonta, J., Gendreau, P., & Cullen, F. T. (1990). Does correctional treatment work? A clinically relevant and psychologically informed meta-analysis. *Criminology, 28*(3), 369-404.

Anglin, M. D., & Hser, Y. (1990). Treatment of drug abuse. In M. Tonry & J. Q. Wilson (Eds.), *Drugs and crime, crime and justice* (Vol. 13, pp. 393-459). Chicago: University of Chicago Press.

Arizona Department of Corrections. (1990). *Annual report.* Phoenix: Author.

Belenko, S., & Dumanovsky, T. (1993). *Special drug courts* (Bureau of Justice Assistance program brief). Washington, DC: U.S. Department of Justice.

Bureau of Justice Statistics. (1991). *Sourcebook of criminal justice statistics 1991.* Washington, DC: Government Printing Office.

Bureau of Justice Statistics. (1993). *Survey of state prison inmates, 1991.* Washington, DC: U.S. Department of Justice.

Davis, R. C., Smith, B. E., & Lurigio, A. J. (1994). Court Strategies to cope with rising drug caseloads. *The Justice System Journal, 17*(1), 1-15.

Dennis, M. L. (1988). *Implementing randomized field experiments: An analysis of criminal and civil justice research.* Unpublished dissertation, Northwestern University, Evanston, IL.

Deschenes, E. P., & Torres, S. (1996, October). *A process evaluation of Los Angeles County drug courts.* Los Angeles: Countywide Criminal Justice Coordination Committee.

Deschenes, E. P., Turner, S., Greenwood, P. W., & Chiesa, J. (1996). *An experimental evaluation of drug testing and interventions for probationers in Maricopa County, Arizona* (DRU-1387-NIJ). Santa Monica, CA: RAND.

Goldkamp, J. S., & Weiland, D. (1993). *Assessing the impact of Dade County's felony drug court* (Final Report). Philadelphia: Crime and Justice Research Institute.

Milkman, R., Beaudin, B. D., Tarmann, K., & Landson, N. (1992). *Drug offenders and the courts: A national assessment.* McLean, VA: The Lazar Institute.

Turner, S. (1997, July 20-23). *Experimental evaluation of drug testing and treatment interventions for probationers in Maricopa County, Arizona.* Paper presented at Meeting the Challenges of Crime and Justice: The Annual Conference on Criminal Justice Research and Evaluation, Washington, DC.

Turner, S., Petersilia, J., & Deschenes, E. P. (1992). Evaluating Intensive Supervision Probation/Parole (ISP) for drug offenders. *Crime and Delinquency, 38*(4), 539-556.

Turner, S., Petersilia, J., & Deschenes, E. P. (1994). The implementation and effectiveness of drug testing in community supervision: Results of an experimental evaluation. In D. MacKenzie & C. Uchida (Eds.), *Drugs and crime: Evaluating public policy initiatives* (pp. 231-252), Thousand Oaks, CA: Sage.

U.S. Department of Commerce. (1992). *Statistical abstract of the United States.* Washington, DC: Government Printing Office.

7. Challenges for Research and Innovation: When Is a Drug Court Not a Drug Court?

John S. Goldkamp

With the establishment of the first treatment drug court in Miami in 1989 and the subsequent diffusion of the model to many locations across the United States since that time, some of its most enthusiastic supporters have seen in the drug court movement key ingredients for a new paradigm for the criminal courts. Taken at face value, the drug model at least suggests that courts can and should address larger problems (root causes) associated with the individuals who are involved in matters making up the criminal caseload—not just decide and process cases. The drug court movement has stirred a debate in and outside of the national judiciary about whether courts should more fully recognize their role as "social service institution of last resort," and develop new strategies and modes of delivering justice in line with that role, or whether they should resist such "hands-on" involvement and reclaim the more traditional and aloof "hands-off" judicial posture. Since the earliest appearances of the drug court strategy in the sites described in earlier chapters of this book, this debate has become more rounded, more supportive of constructive engagement. As the debate shifts to discussion of the nature of this engagement, the lessons to be drawn from the now-many drug court experiments should hold great interest.

No major institutional change—if indeed the drug courts will ultimately be viewed as one—occurs in isolation from larger and more general formative forces. Once occurring, no fundamental change stays the same, its substance fixed in time once and for all. The discussions of early drug courts in this book have helped illustrate that the drug court innovation evolved in particular social, cultural, economic, historical, and political contexts and was fueled by undercurrents felt on the local level that were different from the themes and solutions emphasized in national policy. In part, these courts can be understood as a spinoff of (or, more likely, a reaction to) the War on Drugs at its height (between about 1984 and 1992). National policy at the end of the Reagan years and in the Bush administration focused on interdiction of drug trafficking on the international level and on punitive criminal justice policies on the local level. Emphasis on drug treatment was notably absent and was clearly not favored.

The rationale for developing the original Miami drug court was simple, if not optimistic: Because processing greater volumes of cases faster did not seem to accomplish much (except to overwhelm the justice system's resources), why not try to reduce crime and the criminal caseload by getting offenders involved in drug treatment? As this volume suggests, the story of how that notion was put into operation, of the lessons learned, and of how the idea traveled to jurisdictions across the country is one of the more interesting episodes in American criminal justice innovation in recent times, particularly because it occurred in traditional, change-resistant criminal courts. Above all, the story of the diffusion of the drug court innovation is a story of local problem solving, one that, until recently (1995), occurred without significant federal assistance. In hindsight and with scores of examples now to consider, central themes in the drug court model clearly emerge. However, the transfer of the drug court approach from one jurisdiction to another was not formulaic and did not involve the wholesale export (or import) of some standard, pat model invented in Miami, one-size-fits-all.

One of the striking aspects of the growth of these courts has been the way the concept has spread across the country. Basically, after the first court was established in Miami, judges and other officials began to visit and observe. Soon a small, informal network of courts and judicial officials had been established building on informal contacts and the need for mutual assistance. Literally hundreds of visitors observed the Miami court, once established; the same phenomenon occurred in Oakland, Portland, and Las Vegas and now occurs in most of the established courts. Through visits, observation, and discussion, new courts were designed that borrowed features of various existing courts, while devising special adaptations tailor-made to their own local settings. The knowledge of how to design, implement, and operate a drug court, which resided in this growing but still informal network of judicial professionals, was based on its participants' collective experience and mutual consultation. The path taken by the drug court innovation can be traced through the traffic pattern and volume of visitors to the various courts, first Miami, then Oakland and Portland, Fort Lauderdale, Las Vegas, and, more recently, the Midtown Manhattan community court—which has spearheaded a new generation of innovation in community courts. While national policy was emphasizing and sponsoring other sorts of approaches to problems of drugs and crime, the drug court movement spread quickly because the Miami innovation spoke to the problems and struggles faced in many local court systems on the grassroots level and inadvertently tapped an underlying hunger for alternative solutions felt on the local level nationwide. In fact, the need for practical, local methodologies to address drugs, drug crime, and the drug caseload was so strong that the time was ripe for innovation in many locations. If the Miami courts had not set the first program in place, any one of a number of other jurisdictions would have, with quite likely the same effect.

When Is a Drug Court a Drug Court: Core Elements

As the publication of this volume suggests, even just considering its short history to date (nearing a decade), the innovation and evolution of drug courts raises interesting questions about the nature of courts, treatment, justice, their interrelationships, and their relationships with larger surrounding social service systems. For whatever reasons, research has lagged well behind these developments and the handful of studies have involved comparatively narrow examinations of the drug court phenomena. Yet, as research and commentary begin to focus on the development of treatment drug courts, many interesting questions, some simple, some complex, wait to be addressed.

Analysis of these issues suggests that one might productively start with two: What *is* a drug court really? What is a drug court *not*? Others will follow inexorably, such as: What are the critical elements of the innovation? How do they challenge the traditional role of the criminal courts' and the criminal justice system's involvement with substance abuse and other forms of treatment and service delivery? The Drug Court Resource Center at the American University has begun the task of compiling information describing drug courts as they become known. As this information is being collected and analyzed to outline the features of courts identifying themselves as drug courts, there is still a need to identify common defining elements that make for a treatment drug court. Setting aside the many possible variations in the drug court model, it is at least safe to argue that, at its most compelling, the treatment drug court model—what a "drug court" is—rests on the following minimum elements:

- *A New Substantive Focus on Treatment, With Goals, Values and Methods That Are Nontraditional for the Criminal Court*: Taken most literally, a treatment drug court is a court-centered (court-owned and run) approach to treatment, with new aims and techniques that operate within criminal justice boundaries. (It is not a traditional treatment approach that operates with criminal justice clients who have been referred outside of criminal justice). The drug court has reprioritized processing goals, has focused on treatment progress in a "hands-on" way, has innovated new hearing and enforcement procedures reflecting new aims, and has improvised a new method or style of operation.
- *A New Judicial Role and New Related Roles for Other Players:* In its purest form, this has meant a new judicial role and a new perspective on criminal court proceedings, in which the judge is part adjudicator but also part supervisor and dispenser of treatment. (When Miami's first drug court judge, the Honorable Stanley Goldstein, was once asked "Doesn't that turn the judge into a social worker or probation officer?" the judge simply replied "Yes.") For

the judge, this means dealing with offenders in treatment, having some knowledge of addictive behaviors and a tolerance for initial failures, and adjusting courtroom procedures to correspond to treatment values (within appropriate limits). At the same time, prosecutors and defenders have also adapted their respective roles to support the treatment process, within certain boundaries and agreed upon limits. (It is hard to imagine a treatment drug court that operates without the support of both prosecutors and defense counsel.) Similarly, other support personnel, such as pretrial services, probation, and treatment staff, operate in different ways in the drug court.

• *A Newly Defined Working Relationship Between Treatment and Criminal Courts (and Between the Drug Court and Other Social Services)*: At the heart of the treatment drug court is a newly negotiated working relationship between treatment providers and the criminal court. The drug court does not simply refer cases out to treatment, as in the traditional probation model. Rather, partly out of dissatisfaction with how the probation model has worked, the drug court works out a regimen or range of treatment services that will be provided during the period the court has the defendant or offender under its control. As the drug court model has evolved, this has also meant involvement of related health and social services (such as education, employment, housing, etc.) to strengthen the treatment process and to build strong links to the community and aftercare. Thus, in the drug court, the criminal court has been challenging the substance abuse treatment profession to create a treatment approach that can be effective within criminal justice boundaries, all while linked more accountably to the criminal court judge. Bringing treatment and criminal justice together in the courtroom highlights the differences and possible conflicts in values, goals, and methods of the criminal court and the treatment profession. Add to these incompatibilities the problems of fragmentation, inefficiency, and funding cuts experienced in related social service delivery areas (e.g., the impact of welfare reform). Under the drug court model, these conflicts have to be resolved in a working relationship that is new and comprehensive and that integrates values and features of the respective disciplines in an operating framework acceptable to the criminal court (given the requirements of criminal processing). The drug court framework in turn seeks to produce more effective and appropriate treatment and related support services. The process of defining this working relationship, a work in progress in many of the drug courts and planning sites, raises many of the interesting issues that have to be confronted about treatment, social services, and their relationship to criminal justice and criminal court proceedings.

When Is a Drug Court Not a Drug Court?

In its rapid growth, the drug court movement is and has been presented with the challenge of trying to define the drug court concept. The model of what a drug court is or could be has changed shape from its invention in Miami in 1989 to the other first-generation sites described in this volume and, now, to the many other jurisdictions involved in planning, implementing, and operating new courts. Simultaneously, the task of describing, understanding, and assessing this reform through research has been made more difficult. Capturing the phenomenon of change in this area has become the equivalent of "hitting a moving target," as the original concept has been transformed and become far more complex, branching out to different target populations and different models of court processing and intervention.

The initial, but still as yet unmet, challenge for research relating to treatment drug courts was straightforward and basic:

- What are drug courts and what can we learn about their impact?
- What are the implications of the drug court movement for American courts and criminal justice?

When there were only a handful of treatment drug courts, examination of these types of questions seemed reasonably feasible. But once the genie was released from the lamp, the evolution of drug courts has merged with (stimulated as well as affected by) a larger climate of change in America's courts. This minor sea-change, the duration and full extent of which is currently unknown, is part of a larger change extending beyond criminal courts to encompass surrounding disciplines and social service functions. Given their focus on drug and alcohol treatment, changes in health, managed care, and welfare reform now dramatically affect the design and operation of drug courts as well.

For research, which lags seriously behind these developments, this rapid evolution of form and substance represents a missed opportunity to document and analyze a potentially fundamental innovation as it unfolds and undergoes metamorphoses. Having failed to respond to the initial and more basic questions posed by the drug court phenomenon, research now faces more difficult problems exploring the nature and testing the effects of the change in progress. The farther behind research falls in addressing this critical area of change, the more important a carefully conceived and targeted multisite national research agenda becomes.

With time passing by without a growing body of research to address the questions posed by the rapidly changing drug court movement, we may soon be in a situation analogous to the townspeople in the early television serial left breathing the dust, listening to the receding hoofbeats, and asking "Who was that masked man?" We simply have not learned much from research about the first efforts in local innovation of drug courts and will now be harder put to frame study of successive iterations of the reform while keeping in mind the context of their origins. With more federal funding from two successive crime bills, the rate of development—and of change in the original model—appears to be accelerating exponentially (from 1 or 2 or 3 to something under 300 drug courts in 9 years).

A first problem, then, is that the diffusion of ideas about the court-based innovation has spread faster than empirical knowledge of what has been happening. When we finally learn what we learn, we may learn more about where we've been (which is not unimportant) than about where we are or where we are going in this area.

But a second problem has to do with the diversity in the substance of what a drug court is. This means that research, as it does get moving, will face serious problems of validity, both internal and external, because the nature of the treatment (what the drug court is) being measured is so varied and, often, vague. In an experimental sense, this raises questions about the integrity of the treatment, that is, about the definition and delivery of what "it" is.

Developing a Drug Court Typology

The problem posed by the growing diversity of drug courts is illustrated in Figure 7.1, which identifies elements of drug courts (critical defining dimensions) that could form the basis of a descriptive typology. Drug courts may differ along at least the seven dimension shown in Figure 7.1, relating to the target problem addressed, the population targeted, the court processing focus and stage of intervention, the identification of candidates, the structure

1. *Target Problem*
   Homeless heroin involved
   Drug-related property crime
   Female prostitution-drugs-property crime
   Alcohol and driving
   AOD and domestic violence
   AOD and juvenile crime
   Drugs-mentally ill-property
   Property crime-AOD-HIV/other health
   Community safety, petty offenses, quality of life in geographic area
   AOD and family cases
   AOD and custody
   AOD and divorce

2. *Target Population*
   Misdemeanor cases
   Felony cases
   Juvenile delinquency cases
   Juvenile status cases
   Juvenile dependency and neglect cases
   Domestic violence criminal cases
   Domestic violence civil (protection order) cases
   Female offenders
   Family, custody, divorce cases

3. *Court Processing Focus and Adaptations*
   Diversion
   Probation/parole and revocation
   Incarcerated sentenced to release
   Multiple foci
   Noncriminal areas
   Role of judge (part-time, full-time)
   Role of other actors
   Use of courtroom
   Single court, single judge
   Multicourt, multijudge (within large county, region, state)
   Rural, tribal, urban
   Relation to differentiated case management procedures and larger case processing

4. *Identifying, Screening, and Evaluating Candidates*
   Arrest charges
   Pretrial services screens
   Pre-sentencing
   Pre-release/parole
   Improvised treatment assessment

(Continued)

Figure 7.1. Constructing a Drug Court Typology: Key Defining Dimensions

In-depth evaluation of treatment and related needs
Classification of drug-related defendants/offenders for treatment

5. *Structure and Content of Treatment*
   Structure of program phases, components
   Basic requirements for completion
   Range and nature of modalities
   Single or multiple providers
   Network of treatment options and related support services
   Case management and accountability of treatment system to the drug court
   Specific content and nature of services
   Costs of services
   Funding of treatment and supporting services

6. *Responses to Performance: Client Accountability*
   Incentives/rewards
   Disincentives/sanctions
   Guidelines for termination/completion

7. *Extent of Systemwide Support and Participation*
   Involvement of different actors and agencies in justice, health, and other systems
   Sources of funding
   Integration of services into drug court program

Figure 7.1. (Continued)

and content of treatment, the mechanism employed to assure compliance with the program, and the extent of system-wide support.

1. *Target Problem*: Jurisdictions do differ in the specific drug-crime problem that has motivated them to go to the trouble of designing and implementing a drug court, ranging from homelessness and heroin addiction in South Central Los Angeles to quality of life misdemeanor crimes, such as prostitution and theft, in Midtown Manhattan.

2. *Target Population:* Drug courts have opted to focus on a diverse collection of target populations when viewed across the country, from misdemeanor and felony drug defendants, to domestic violence defendants, felony probationers, probation and parole revokees, female offenders, and juvenile offenders.

3. *Court Processing Focus and Adaptations:* Courts have elected to intervene with drug court candidates at various stages of processing, from shortly after arrest to sentencing and revocation. Courts differ in how the drug court is integrated into other court processing and/or case-flow management functions, in the geographic area covered by the court, and in administrative approaches taken in the courts.

4. *Identification, Screening, and Evaluation of Candidates:* Courts differ in the rough criteria and procedures they employ to locate and enroll drug court candidates and in the use of clinical assessments to evaluate the substance abuse involvement of candidates once located.

5. *Structure and Content of Treatment:* The type of treatment programs associated with drug courts, the range of options for treatment, the substance of treatment services provided, as well as the types of supporting services, program phases, graduation requirements, and means of funding treatment, also differentiate drug courts across the nation.

6. *Responses to Performance: Client Accountability:* Drugs courts were developed in part to establish greater accountability for participants than was usually the case under other models of treatment in criminal justice. They differ in the kinds of responses they employ to reward positive achievement in treatment and to discourage poor performance (i.e., encourage compliance).

7. *Extent of System-Wide Support:* Drug courts differ in the type of support and participation they have built in from other criminal justice system actors and from representatives of health, treatment, and other important social service delivery fields outside of justice.

Even if this list correctly narrows down key defining dimensions of the drug court model and its variations to seven main dimensions, the diversity and complexity of possible variation is easily demonstrated. Given this diversity, the challenge for research is to understand both the principal components of the drug court model and its variations as practiced across the country and to investigate the impact of these structural features. Classification of drug court sites on these dimensions using such a working typology will quickly show how courts differ in important, structural details and how generalizations about drug courts will need to be qualified as particular examples are considered. The bottom line is that without more specific definition of what a drug court is, we will learn less through research about the importance and impact of specific elements that make up the collection of court innovations known as drug courts.

The Challenge for Research

The problem for internal validity is to try to determine the impact of a particular version of drug court on agreed-upon local outcome measures. Without an understanding of the operational elements making up a specific example of drug court, examination of the relationship between the treatment (what the specific drug court is) and outcomes will be difficult, as it will be difficult to report on what about a particular drug court appears to "work." If there is a positive outcome in a particular site, what about that particular drug court approach explains that outcome? Unless research begins to build knowledge of which features of drug courts explain their performance and how they manage to have their impact, then comparison of the drug court model across sites becomes very difficult indeed. The more vague the notion of the treatment in one site and the more varied the approaches of other sites, the more challenging the questions that must be confronted in research evaluations about external validity and whether the drug court model (whatever it is) can be replicated across settings. Does the drug court model work in other very different settings or does it work in a very different form—if so or if not, why? And, if it did, would "it" still be what we mean when we think of a "drug court?"

This concern with the application and transformation of the innovation (the changing and adapting treatment) from setting to setting is important for another reason—the high priority given to research using experimental designs by potential funders of evaluations. The emphasis by funders on evaluation through field experimentation rather than less rigorous designs is understandable. There is a well-known and difficult history in criminal justice evaluation generally, which has been characterized by a lack of rigorous and replicable field experiments (see, e.g., Martinson and the "Nothing Works" controversy regarding rehabilitation). However, without resolving questions about the integrity of the treatment—of what it is that the drug court is—field experiments will suffer from problems of internal validity in individual studies and will certainly not provide answers to questions about the impact of the innovation as it is replicated across sites. When you evaluate Court A with certain attributes and Court B with certain others, what are we learning about drug courts in a collective sense?

This issue is more complicated when, in this instance, a great many of the questions about the integrity of the treatment have to do with the content and delivery of substance abuse treatment in treatment drug courts. To the extent that drug treatment is the main component of the treatment (in the experimental sense), there are many questions to be answered about the content of what is being delivered to participants—in the same location over time and, particularly in jurisdictions across the country.

Questions about the integrity of treatment in examining drug courts can be salient to understanding the drug court in one jurisdiction over time as well as in research focusing on individual and multiple sites at a given moment in time. What does what the drug court was in Miami in 1989 or in Portland in 1991 have to do with what the respective courts are now in those sites in 1997? In one place over time—in those sites with long-enough histories, such as Miami, Portland, and Oakland—has the innovation, (the drug court model or the treatment) remained constant over time? Such stability and consistency over time would be highly unlikely. The issues raised in individual jurisdictions parallel issues raised by cross-jurisdictional comparisons we may wish to make:

What do the results from the study of the probation court in Phoenix (Deschenes & Petersen, Chapter 6, this volume) have to do with the study of the diversion court in Miami (Goldkamp, Chapter 2, this volume) and the study of the multi-track District of Columbia drug court (Harrell & Cavanaugh, 1996)?

What do these studies say about the nature and impact of the drug court innovation, its development, the power of its essential ingredients, and its meaning for the courts and justice system overall as the innovation shifts into noncriminal areas, such as domestic violence, juvenile justice, and family court matters?

What then is the answer to the question, When is a drug court not a drug court? For now, it is difficult to say in any strict sense. With few single-site studies and no multi-site investigations available to date, research offers little help in establishing a common, larger framework describing what a drug court is in specific terms. We are not yet at the stage of seeing what the boundaries of the innovation may be, what the fundamental components are, or more important, what effect these ingredients may have separately or taken together. That agenda for research still lies ahead.

References

Harrell, A., & Cavanaugh, S. (1996, November). *Early intervention with drug felony defendants: Findings from the D.C. Superior Court drug intervention program.* Paper presented at the meetings of the American Society of Criminology, Chicago.

Martinson, R. (1974). What works? Questions and answers about prison reform. *The Public Interest, 35,* 22-54.

Index

About the Editor

W. **Clinton Terry, III** is Associate Professor in the Criminal Justice program at Florida International University. He holds a PhD in sociology from the University of California at Santa Barbara and was a DAAD Fellow at the University of Göttingen, Germany. He previously taught criminology and criminal justice at the California State University at Fresno and at the University of Florida. He has written articles on a wide variety of police topics, mostly focusing upon the organization of police departments and behavior of officers. He has also participated in and directed research about prison use in Florida, bail bond and pretrial release in Dade County, Florida's State Certification Examination for Law Enforcement and Correctional Personnel, and criminal patterns in Opa Locka, Florida. He has conducted evaluations of the Miami Police Department's Crimes Against the Elderly Unit, the DARE program in Broward County, Florida, and the Broward County Drug Court. The last project resulted in the appearance of this edited volume.

About the Contributors

Brooke Bedrick is Deputy Research Director at the Police Foundation, and a PhD student in the jurisprudence and social policy program at the University of California, Berkeley. She has an MA in history from Columbia University and a BA in anthropology from Harvard University, where she was elected to Phi Beta Kappa. She has worked with young people on parole from the California Youth Authority and has provided literacy tutoring to women in the San Francisco Jail. She is the author of *Improving Treatment Services for Drug Court Clients in Alameda and Contra Costa Counties,* a report published for the East Bay Public Safety Corridor Partnership. She is interested in the social and historical construction of justice, the history of punishment, and the gender, race, and class dimensions of the administration of justice.

Steven Belenko is Senior Research Associate at the National Center on Addiction and Substance Abuse at Columbia University. He received his bachelor's degree in applied mathematics and PhD in experimental psychology from Columbia University. He has held senior research positions at the New York City Criminal Justice Agency, Inc., the New York City Mayor's Criminal Justice Coordinating Council, Mathematica Policy Research, and the Vera Institute of Justice. He has directed research projects on various topics related to drugs and the criminal justice system. He has been studying drug courts since 1991. His other research interests include HIV risks and risk prevention, sexual violence and substance abuse, and access to treatment services. His book, *Crack and the Evolution of Anti-Drug Policy,* was published in 1993 and received an Outstanding Academic Book Award from the American Library Association's *Choice Magazine.*

Elizabeth Piper Deschenes is Professor at California State University, Long Beach, in the Department of Criminal Justice. She received her bachelor's degree in sociology from Colby College and both an MA and a PhD in criminology from the University of Pennsylvania. Previously, she worked for URSA Institute on the Violent Juvenile Offender Project and for UCLA's Drug Abuse Research Center on studies of narcotics addicts. As a consultant to RAND since 1986, she has been involved in evaluations of experimental correctional programs for adults and juveniles, including intensive supervision programs for different types of drug offenders, residential and intensive aftercare programs for juvenile delinquents, and court-supervised drug testing and treatment for adult probationers. She is currently working on evaluations of adult drug courts in Los Angeles and Orange Counties, as well as a study of a drug court for juveniles in Los Angeles County.

John S. Goldkamp is Professor of Criminal Justice at Temple University and heads the Crime and Justice Research Institute, a nonprofit research organization in Philadelphia. He has studied bail practices in the United States for two decades, producing numerous reports, articles, and books. Recent work has focused on innovation in the courts and, in particular, the growth of treatment drug courts and the application of the drug court treatment concept to domestic violence. His study of the Miami Drug Court was published at the end of 1993, and the directions and implications of the movement were described in *Justice and Treatment Innovation: The Drug Court Movement*. He conducted a National Institute of Justice study of Miami's domestic violence court *(The Role of Drugs and Alcohol Abuse in Domestic Violence and Its Treatment: Dade County's Domestic Violence Court Experiment)*. His focus on the evolving role of criminal courts is reflected in a project to establish comprehensive alternatives to incarceration and effective management of jail overcrowding in Philadelphia. He is conducting evaluations of drug courts in Philadelphia, Portland, and Las Vegas, and evaluating Philadelphia's Criminal Justice Treatment Network for Women.

Rebecca D. Petersen is Assistant Professor of Criminal Justice in the Division of Social and Policy Sciences at the University of Texas San Antonio. She received her bachelor's degree cum laude in criminal justice from Northeast Missouri State University and both her MS and PhD in Justice Studies from Arizona State University. Her research interests include adult and juvenile corrections, juvenile justice, women and crime, and public policy. She has worked on several research projects funded by the National Institute of Justice, the U.S. Department of Education, the Arizona Department of Corrections, the Arizona Institute for Criminal Justice, and the Arizona Department of Youth Treatment and Rehabilitation, and she has been a consultant to RAND.

Jerome H. Skolnick is Claire Clements Dean Professor Emeritus at the University of California at Berkeley, adjunct professor of law at New York University School of Law, and codirector of the Center for Research in Crime and Justice. Recently, he served as chair of the National Academy of Science's Committee on Law and Justice, and he is a past president of the American Society of Criminology. He is the author of numerous articles on police, courts, and criminal justice policy. His work, *Justice Without Trial: Law Enforcement in a Democratic Society* (1966) is now a scholarly classic. *Politics of Protest* (1969) was perhaps his most widely read book, selling several hundred thousand paperback copies. His *The New Blue Line* (1986) inspired the present volume.